Ivan Antic

AWAKENING

THE UNITY OF THE OUTER AND INNER WORLDS

SAMKHYA PUBLISHING LTD
London, 2023

Translated by
James Joshua Pennington, PhD

Proofreading & editing by
Joel R. Dennstedt

Copyright © 2023 by SAMKHYA PUBLISHING LTD
All rights reserved.
ISBN: 9798392681051

In memory of
Peter Bronzan
1987-2022, Dubrovnik

To all the confused souls
who are searching everywhere for that very light
that they've carried inside themselves all along

Table of Contents

Prologue	7
Testimonies about the unity of the outer and inner worlds	8
What is really *inner*?	
What then is the *outer* universe?	14
Beginning of unity recognition inner and outer	17
Perfect rest and perfect action together bring awakening	21
Dream and reality are one and the same neither is an illusion	28
The exact definition of awakening and unconsciousness	35
The basis of consciousness	39
Space is currently creating everything that exists	42
The physics of the inner and outer world	48
The connection of the outer and the inner through the human	53
Nature awakens us	55
Love awakens us	59
Awakening is necessary even if everything is divine consciousness	63
Developing a culture of recognition of the outer world as human essence	65
Why the outside world has a conditioning effect on us	68
How the division began	73
Everywhere there is a combination of outer and inner	75
Religion is a reflection of unity inner and outer	76
Astrology is the science of unity the inner and outer world	78

Birth and dying is a twist of the inner and outer	84
Between the outer and the inner is where the dimensions of nature are located	89
Nature is already awake, only people are sleeping	93
How to recognize an awakened human	99
How the awakened person sees the world	109
How do we become awake when the passions are so strong	112
Awakening is beyond time and space	116
Awakening happens in time and space	119
Kindness harmonizes the outer and inner worlds	123
Meditation is a direct combination of inner and outer	125
The development of science and culture is an indirect connection of inner and outer	126
We rule the outer world only as much we rule ourselves	129
Here's the good news: we can never be at a loss	130
Dream or reality - human or butterfly	136
In out-of-body experiences, we do not leave ourselves	137
Practical exercises for sanctifying the exterior as one's own being	140
Understanding the meaning of merging the outer and inner world	157
Some more technical details about awakening	160
Sudden and gradual awakening	165
Individual and collective awakening	169
Does everyone need to wake up	181
Epilogue	186

Prologue

"What you don't know is that the whole Universe is your body and you don't need to be scared of it. One could say that there are two bodies: the human and the universal. The human comes and goes, the universal stays with you.

The total creation is your universal body. You are so blinded by what is human that you cannot see what is universal. This delusion cannot be discarded as is - it must be overcome with great skill and care. When all the deceptions have become understandable, comprehended, and fulfilled, you will reach a state free from delusion, a perfect state in which there is no difference between the human and the universal. Knowing yourself as a resident in both bodies, you do not renounce anything. The Universe is your concern, your interest, every living thing you will love and help in the most gentle and wise way. There shall be no conflict of interest between you and others. All abuse will end. Your every action will be useful, your every action will be blessed."

Sri Nisargadatta Maharaj

TESTIMONIES ABOUT THE UNITY OF THE OUTER AND INNER WORLDS

The lives of all of us, all the mental, cultural, spiritual, and civilizational maturation of humans is based on the awareness of the true nature and relationship of the inner and outer worlds, on the understanding of our human essence and the cosmos. The pinnacle of spiritual knowledge is the recognition of the complete unity of the outer and inner cosmos.

If we identify the outer universe as God, then we can easily see how strong and universal has been the desire throughout human history to understand the true relationship between the outer and the inner. This is most directly manifested in the words that God is within us and that God is "our father in heaven". We have always seen him in the heavens and felt him in ourselves, in our essence, "in our hearts".

According to the words of Jesus from the *Gospel of Thomas 1:22*: "When you make the two into one, and when you make the inner like the outer and the outer like the inner, and the upper like the lower... then you will enter the Kingdom of Heaven."

From the amazed faces of the first people to look up towards the heavens, through the statement that "the kingdom of heaven is within us and all around us" [1], to the modern discovery that the images of the most distant universe we have managed to reach with radio telescopes are completely identical to the microscopic images of the neurons of our brain – there has always been the idea that the outer universe is an inseparable part of our innermost

---

[1] The Gnostic Gospel of Thomas.

being, and this is the foundation of spirituality, science and mysticism.

If we were to enumerate the works that deal in most detail with witnessing the unity of the outer and inner universe, then we would certainly have to single out the most famous works of mysticism in the East: the Vedas, Upanishads, and Bhagavad Gita, which tell us that they are awake "who see all beings in themselves and themselves in all beings". The Avadhuta Gita, Ashtavakra Gita, Ribhu Gitaspeak directly about the unity of our innermost Self or soul (*atman*) with the essence of the universe (*brahman*). The messages of all these works were summarized by Adi Shankara in the teachings of *Advaita Vedanta*, which in its entirety says there is no duality or division between those two apparent extremes or dualities of us and the universe, the outer and the inner. When Ramana Maharshi said that "a man's true greatness begins where he (as an individual, the ego) ceases to exist," he meant the absolute reality of humans.

The works of Buddhism also speak about this, but in a more direct way; that is, exclusively from the point of view of practice and without getting lost in metaphysical discussions or beliefs that satisfy only feelings or religious convictions. In addition to the Buddha's speeches, such experience is also and perhaps best expressed in the work of Nagarjuna (*Mula madhyamaka karika*). He directly exposed the nature of the objective world as emptiness; that is, he removed any quality of substantiality from the external manifested world in order to open a path for understanding that the entire external universe is actually our own being (our buddha nature), that the external is not at all different from us, that we should not even entertain the notion there is anything outside or different from our perceiving consciousness. The world does not exist as something real in itself on the outside, because everything is just one being, and that being is our self. The consciousness in us that perceives the world is the same consciousness that currently makes up the world. Awakening occurs when we discover within ourselves the unity of consciousness as subject and object. When we realize this, the illusion of our own birth and existence evaporates, including any illusion that our individuality exists by itself as separate from the outer world.

Of all these spiritual practices and traditions, *Samkhya theory* is the oldest. It precedes all in age and originality. All other approaches use it as their foundation. *Samkhya* directly teaches that the entire external universe, called *prakrti*, is only a mirror or manifested aspect of the absolute consciousness or *purusha* that is our essence or soul. We are born into our body, see the outer world as real, and live in this world with all its karmic drama only when we remain unaware of our true nature, our essence or soul. Just as we always exist when we dream and when we are awake, so our essence - soul or *purusha* - always exists intact, independent of the apparent world, but still always accessible to us. It is never truly threatened, enslaved or freed from suffering—no more than in a dream. It's just about awakening. **Awakening is the only thing that can happen to a person in this world. Nothing else can or does happen to them, because all that happens is prakrti.**

Understanding the differences and the unity of the inner and outer universe is the essence of spiritual traditions in the West. It is expressed above all else in hermeticism, which has its source in the works of Hermes Trismegistos or Thoth. The basic principle of hermeticism is succinctly expressed in the following words: *As below, so above; and as above so below. As it is within, so it is without; as it is outside, so it is inside. As it is in the great, so it is in the small.*

The second point of the writings of the *Emerald Tablet* reads: *As below, so above; and as above so below. With this knowledge alone you may work miracles.*

Here we are talking about the human essence or soul that rises to the sky and descends to the earth, that tests the inner and outer state in order to absorb the strength of the upper and lower world, and thus to master all existence.

"Working miracles" is essentially the final act of the differentiation process, the manifestation of the cosmos. It happens only in an awakened person. In order to reach the experience of union, the experience of separation is necessary; the easy must be separated from the difficult, distinguishing everything for the sake of understanding, while naming all things and phenomena for the sake of establishment. It is the analytical method of inner alchemy with which one masters the elements of nature and becomes perfect. That is why Hermeticism is the basis of alchemy and why alchemy is the basis of modern science. Science, then, is the perfect means for expression of soul consciousness.

However, these works have been distorted or concealed over time, probably waiting for the right time to reveal their full content. The time of their discovery is the main theme of the history of the human race, which takes place through the development of culture and civilization.

In the East, the experience of the inner world, the human essence, was preserved to a greater extent but not sufficiently expressed externally. In the West, the external discovery of the world was to a greater extent expressed but insufficiently integrated with the inner essence of humankind. Namely, we are awakening to the realization of the true nature of the outer world. This knowledge develops through the development of science and technology. Through the development of science, one manifests consciousness of their soul and better understands their soul, as well as the external universe or nature itself. Humans still do not understand that through scientific knowledge of the outer world they actually come to know their essence. They still look at the world through science as something outside, separate from themselves, even denying the soul. Only in recent times, through a better understanding of quantum physics and environmental awareness, is there realization of the connection between the outer and inner world and a growing holistic approach to scientific development. This promises that science will develop in the right direction - towards self-knowledge.

The contemporary understanding of the universe as a hologram[2] is closest to the understanding we are talking about here: the unity of the outer and inner world. To say that the universe is a hologram, that every bit of the universe contains a reflection of the entire universe, is just another way of saying what we are saying here: that our essence is the universe itself.

For cognition of the outer world to take place perfectly and correctly through science and technology, it must first have its foothold within the human being; it must start from within. Science connects the inner and outer universe. When science does not have the human soul as its basis, it is destructive. The better a person knows their inner self, the more they will be able to cor-

---

[2] See the book Michael Talbot: *The Holographic Universe: The Revolutionary Theory of Reality.*

rectly know the outer universe. That is why science of the future will either be based on meditation or will not exist.

WHAT IS REALLY *INNER*?
WHAT THEN IS THE *OUTER* UNIVERSE?

First of all, we need to clarify the meaning of the terms we are talking about.

When we say 'inner world', we can easily understand that it comprises all our psychological life, mind, feelings, memories, personal subconscious that is individual in every person, and deep collective unconscious with archetypal content that is common to all people. Some parts of that inner world are studied by psychology. A unique property of the inner world is that we access it only through personal experience; it manifests as personal experience, which often cannot be perfectly expressed on the outside, not even in words. That is why misunderstandings often arise. In short, the 'inner world' refers to everything that is bounded by the physical body, primarily the psyche.

The external universe is everything that is outside the body and is common to all conscious beings. It is the physical world in which we all live and whose experience we all have in common, and whose properties we can all agree on. The so-called natural sciences deal with the study of the properties of the outer world.

Recently, the oldest science of nature, physics, went deep enough to discover that the fundamental properties of nature at the finest subatomic level in the microcosm behave very similarly to our inner world, learning that its elements are connected independently of external time and space (the macrocosm), just as thoughts and memories are connected in us as an independent whole. In short, we can think about the past, present, and future. In fact, it was discovered that the presence of a conscious subject itself affects the results of experiments studying the behavior of subatomic particles. It is as if the manifestation of the external physical world directly depends on the internal one and they are consciously connected through humans. In fact, this is experimental proof of the unity of the outer and inner cosmos and our role in that unity. It has not been officially confirmed yet; only theories about it are permitted.

Ancient esoteric science confirmed long ago the existence of different dimensions in nature. External nature is not a one-dimensional entity in which we live, but in addition to gross physical forms, it also has other, finer dimensions. That ancient science remained esoteric because it immediately discovered that these higher dimensions are also within human beings, that humans are made up of all the dimensions of nature. The highest dimension of nature, the world of ideas, is the mental world in humans, their ability to think and remember. The lowest dimension of nature is the physical world of forms; it is the human body. That is why humans can be aware of all nature and the meaning of all its processes, all events. As if humans are the place where the outer and inner cosmos intersect, all dimensions of nature come to awareness of themselves in humans. On the outside, they are just preparing for this. The outer world is therefore only the preparation of details necessary for connection as the awareness that occurs in human self-realization. The outer world is only a stage for playing out the drama of divine self-realization through humans.

The world around us is inherently structured to facilitate the acquisition of a wide range of experiences from all perspectives. Consider the construction and habitation of a house over many years, which presents numerous opportunities for varied experiences. Though subject to entropy, the house will remain relatively consistent in its existence and location while also being capable of modification to suit our changing needs. This stability ensures that it can serve as a vehicle for experiencing a wide range of phenomena. This quality is intrinsic to the physical world. In contrast, higher dimensions do not permit this extended, multi perspective experience, since everything is instantaneous in those realms.

BEGINNING OF UNITY RECOGNITION
INNER AND OUTER

The key moment for realizing the unity of inner and outer occurs during meditation. From here, one must begin their understanding of this unity. Meditation is the complete calming of body and mind. In complete calm, the complete unity of consciousness and existence is revealed. Any difference between our consciousness and being, between the inner and outer world, between our deepest feeling of "I am" and existence itself - disappears. Then, we exist more strongly than ever, and we are more aware of ourselves than ever.

In that moment of complete union, we realize that our being and the outer world disappear when the mind is calm and consciousness rests within itself as pure wakefulness. That is why meditation is a complete and time-controlled renunciation of the world and existence. The body, feelings, and mind disappear, and only existence without limits remains, which we experience as our essence. To experience this even for a moment is the purpose of meditation.

The key moment of insight occurs after one breaks their rest in meditation. Then, one can clearly see their awareness of the body, sensation, and mind return. But in the background, there remains that sense of rest in transcendental consciousness. For a moment, one remains double: inside still calm, even while the movement of body and mind occur outside as one remains immobile inside

Calming oneself in meditation comes down to narrowing one's attention to the subject itself, to the pure feeling of presence in oneself, to resting in the "I am." Turning attention inward begins with witnessing the whole body and mind, with a constant turning toward oneself to the one who is aware of everything. When that witness becomes stronger, when it becomes rid of the illusion that it must identify with those objects it witnesses, meditation matures and one realizes that the witness can exist without the objects it witnesses, without body or thoughts, simply as a pure presence within oneself somewhere behind the eyes. This insight reaches its peak with the realization that the witness has always been independent of everything else. One's identification with objects was only a dream; one's recognition of their true nature as the independent witness is an awakening.

But it does not end there. One clearly sees that all activities of the body and mind are not different or separate from the witness, from pure transcendental consciousness, that pure existence as "I am" that one experiences during complete stillness (samadhi). One sees that consciousness (the transcendental witness) begins to vibrate as a thought, then begins to vibrate as a feeling, then vibrates as a body and the body's movements. This is certainly not areal "vibration" of consciousness, but rather its imagined vibration. One sees that pure self-awareness is transformed into thought, feeling, body, and movement - into existence. One sees that there is no difference between consciousness and the forms consciousness takes in its various vibrations. All forms of existence are but the imagination of self-consciousness. One becomes one self when pure consciousness (our Self, *atman* or soul) becomes thought, feeling, body, and all body movements. One vibrates into being as thought, feeling, and body. One is, in essence, the very existence that vibrates as everything that manifests.

Nor does it end there, either. Before the creation of one's body and life as we know it, consciousness of our soul - the divine consciousness - produced in just this way the cosmos itself in all its dimensions.

The mind is actually a mechanism that makes artificial distinctions between consciousness/existence and thoughts, bodies, and everything else. In objective reality, the subject and object, observer and observed, are one and the same thing. ***A dream or illusion arises when subject and object seem to differ.*** Because in reality the separation of subject and object does not exist, this is possible only in the imagination, in the mind, in a dream-like state. The mind is the mechanism that creates a difference, but it also recognizes the unity. Therefore, it is the same mechanism that both separates and unites existence and consciousness. It puts us to sleep and it wakes us up. There is, in truth, no duality.

In truth, our soul consciousness creates everything, including our thoughts, bodies, and the entire natural world. When we distinguish our consciousness as a separate entity from the vibrations it produces, we fall into the illusion that we are separate individuals in a world fundamentally different from our inner selves. However, this separation is only a dream, for we can never be truly separate in reality. When we dream of separateness, we lose touch with heavenly unity, and we experience conflict, alienation, and loneliness. That's why life is often seen as just a dream.

To reconcile ourselves with the world around us, we must recognize our experiences as simply our own vibrations. We observe this in a state of meditative calm or samadhi. Just like strings on a musical instrument remain the same whether they are vibrating or at rest, we too are always the same in our essence, the difference being only in our vibrations. Similarly, a dancer and their dance are inseparable, with the dance only existing when the dancer is in motion. The dancer creates the dance just as the instrument creates the music, but we tend to focus on the creation rather than the creator.

The first step towards awakening is recognizing our thoughts and experiences as simply creations, rather than reality itself. Permanent awakening comes when we stop distinguishing between our being and its creations, between the manifest and the unmanifest, between the absolute and the relative, and between the inner and the outer. Only then can we create and live our lives fully, playing the instrument of our being in all its tones and rhythms. Awakening is not about denying the world or leaving it behind, but rather understanding it correctly and participating in it from a place of deep awareness.

PERFECT REST AND PERFECT ACTION TOGETHER BRING AWAKENING

The outer and inner world will become one and the same for us when resting in meditation (samadhi) and our activity in the world become one and the same, without any differences.

One cannot be at peace (samadhi) without understanding the true nature of the world and the activities in the world. Because people have the illusion of the world as real, external, and separate from them, they are committed to participating in such a world and considering it the only real life. To some, meditative rest seems like the opposite state, as if one were abandoning life, and therefore such rest is unacceptable. This is the result of illusion and ignorance, both in oneself and in the world.

The perfect rest of the whole being in samadhi is only an apparent abandonment of activity in the world, because in reality there is nothing to abandon; the whole universe is one's being. People first project the illusion that real life requires the isolation of a body in an outside world different from them, and then they fear losing such a small, isolated life. By remaining still, they only abandon the appearance and illusion that the activity of an isolated individual in an alienated world is the real life. In reality, activity in such a world is the only real death one can have.

When the abandonment of the world in the complete stillness of being (samadhi) becomes as dear and as close to people as their activity in the world, which they consider their life, they will awaken to the unity of the outer and inner worlds.

Then they will have both right samadhi and right activity in the world. It is impossible to have only one. Both go together: perfect abandonment of the world, and perfect action in the world.

When people are fully prepared to leave this world, to die at any moment, and to participate perfectly in the life of each moment, then they will awaken - for wakefulness embraces both life and death equally and transcends them.

One cannot be alert if they avoid or attach themselves to anything. This means that reality is an unconditioned whole in which there are no divisions. Awakening happens when one recognizes such an unconditioned whole as their essence.

If one is not able to completely detach from this world at any moment, and if all their passions bind them to acting in the world, it means that they have not understood the true nature of the world, their being, or the true nature of humility. Without such understanding, one cannot function properly in the world. Indeed, a person can never act correctly in the world if they do not experience the world as their own being.

In reality, the outer and inner worlds are one and the same; they have never been separate except within our illusion. This illusion ends with meditative rest. Simply put, cessation of activity in the outer world shatters the illusion of that world. Stop participating in the illusion, and you will wake up.

As a person awakens through meditative rest (samadhi), the same happens in the physics of the micro and macro worlds. The manifested macro world we see in space and time is based on a micro world, the universal quantum field in which everything that is manifested as a multitude in time and space is gathered into One beyond time and space. Unmanifested and manifested are one and the same. The quantum field or ether is the universal space itself in which everything exists. There are no separate things or objects in space, but space itself is instantly compressed and manifested into the form of everything that exists, including every object. In other words, the quantum field or ether is currently manifesting as everything that is manifested - as the world we see.

Let's put this even more simply. When physicists first split the atom, they came to smaller and smaller parts, to subatomic particles. When they got to the smallest, only the clear space in which they existed was left. They called that space the quantum field. Then, they discovered that subatomic particles behave paradoxically within that space, as if instantly appearing and disappearing in it. Only when these particles combine into larger elements do they behave according to the laws of nature known to us.

The same thing happens in meditation, which consists of witnessing. In meditation, we witness everything that happens inside us, from our body and breathing, to feelings, states of mind, and expressions of will (to do some movement or action), to witnessing the very origin of every thought. This is not a static witnessing, but a dynamic, constant witnessing; we go always beyond, ever deeper and finer. In meditation, we bear witness to the witness itself; as long as there is anything to witness, we bear witness to it, including the witness itself. When there is nothing left to witness, then we are truly within ourselves as - our true nature. We become the space in which everything happens, and we are at the same time everything that happens. There is no difference between the subject who bears witness and the object about which they bear witness. It is all one; the same space manifests itself as subject and object, witness and witnessed. Transcendental consciousness, when considered as space, becomes analogous to the quantum field. Just as scientists split the atom and came to empty space (the quantum field), so the meditator through witnessing comes to an ever deeper level of being, to the source of thoughts themselves, and ultimately to the void that makes every thought possible and reveals space in its true essence as self-awareness.

It's all one and the same, just in two aspects: the implicit and the explicit order of one and the same thing. The difference is only in the way we observe and experience. A person is a microcosm. When they rest in samadhi, they actualize the consciousness of the microcosm or the quantum field, the physics of the ether. When they are active in the world, they participate in that same quantum field, but only in its external, manifested aspect; that is, they actualize the consciousness of the macrocosm.

A person can carry out both actualizations - of the micro and macro cosmos; to be at rest and active - because the two only appear as separate in their illusion, and therefore they can merge with the disappearance of that illusion. That's why meditative rest is awakening, while activity is sleep. People move between sleep and waking, between the outer and inner world, as long as there is even the slightest difference between them. Perfect stillness removes all such difference.

What happens in the microcosm and macrocosm, as the unmanifested and the manifested world, happens spontaneously in us both while we rest in a deep and dreamless sleep and when we are active in waking life. So, every day and night we spontaneously move between these two apparent extremes. When we truly awaken, then everything turns around for us: what seemed like reality will now be like a dream, and our state of deep dreamless sleep will now be a state of pure reality - the unity of everything. Deep dreamless sleep is like samadhi but happens spontaneously; therefore, we are not aware of its true nature and we remain unconscious. Awakening occurs when we become fully aware and understand all the states we previously experienced spontaneously and naturally but unconsciously.

In all our changing states, we exist always to bear witness to them. We awaken when our awareness matches the existence that exists always, realizing that as a witness we remain independent of all such changing states of existence.

When at meditative rest (samadhi), we exist at the base of all things and phenomena - at the very center of our being. Then we contain all things within ourselves as their source. When active only in the world, we exist on the periphery of being in a relative state. We gain or lose, are up or down, sometimes rise and sometimes fall. Existence can be compared to a point in the center of a wheel. When we are perfectly aligned with the movement of the whole wheel, we are always at the center of existence. **We experience this center of existence as our center.** When on the wheel's edge, we identify with the outside world, and objects retain a decisive influence on us. Then, we exist in a relative state of ups and downs, where sometimes the wheel of life carries us to the top, and sometimes it tramples us beneath its weight.

When in the center, we exist within the universal quantum field, the quantum mind, and the frequency of our energy body is stationary or non-Hertzian, independent and complete as a sphere. Since we are a holographic being, we experience the hologram whole within ourselves, filled with everything, above all the meaning of everything, experiencing our state as absolute. The center is everywhere. In that state, there is no loss, only fulfillment and bliss. It is a state of complete freedom; since the center is everywhere, there are no objects with their influences in it. We have been looking for such a state all our lives. That search has been the hidden motive for everything we have ever done or strived for. All our lives revolve around it. That state is what we here call: soul consciousness.

The mind is designed to navigate only the periphery of the wheel of life – which represents the relative world. This should be clearly understood. The mind will never allow us to turn from the periphery to the center because it always sees only the periphery - the world as something outside. The mind has nothing to look for inside, in the center of being, because there is no need inside for questions and answers. Everything is already there, nothing hidden, and everything is the answer itself.

On the periphery, we are constantly born and die; the center is eternal life. The mind constantly keeps us in the illusion that real life happens on the periphery (away from the center point) of existence. We don't see that this is actually the real death. However, we should not conclude that the mind is bad and wrong in itself, only that we use it wrongly. The mind is not created to look behind itself, towards the very source of consciousness, but only outside, just like an eye. But just as we cannot see the world without the eye, we also cannot see the world without the mind. Turning to look behind the mind cannot be carried out by any mental effort, but only by meditative stillness or discipline. Stillness of the whole being becomes a practical act of mind transcendence.

What transpires during the moment of complete relaxation known as samadhi? We relinquish ourselves entirely to the totality of our being, including everything that was previously perceived as external or foreign, both the beautiful or desirable and the hostile. We now experience all of it as our being, just as we experience our physical body. Previously, our being was limited to the body alone, but now the boundaries of the body dissolve, and everything is our being. We realize that all the life we possess is derived from the whole, not merely from the air we inhale, but from the space itself that constitutes our existence. We discover the infinite divine love of the whole that always safeguards and sustains us in every conceivable way, even though we were unable to perceive it before. However, divine love cannot reach us if we are trapped in an illusory body and mind; we must vanish in order to truly exist.

The experience of the dissolution of our being's limitations is akin to surrendering to the divine. However, in true surrender, we do not submit to any specific deity; instead, we return to our divine essence. Surrender to the divine and self-realization are not polar opposites, but rather two parts of the same journey. There are no longer any projections outside oneself, not even onto the divine, since there is nothing external anymore. Our consciousness is existence itself, and existence itself is our consciousness. There is nothing that is not divine, and nothing that is not our being.

We vanish into the unity of our divine being. We cannot claim that we have surrendered or achieved self-realization if we continue to exist in the same way as before. Surrender and self-realization are the dispelling of all illusions about oneself. The one who genuinely surrenders and realizes the self is no longer.

DREAM AND REALITY ARE ONE AND THE SAME NEITHER IS AN ILLUSION

The manifestation of thoughts and dreams arises from a yearning to comprehend or create meaning in our existence. However, upon achieving true enlightenment, such mental constructs become obsolete. They are recognized as mere reflections of reality, **and all external phenomena are but realized thoughts and dreams**. As such, there is no need to repeat them in our minds for the sake of understanding, for we see things as they are - unfiltered and direct.

The objective world that exists externally is a representation of the same consciousness that exists within us, giving rise to our awareness of the world. Thus, we are omnipresent, differing only in the quality of our vibration. This is the crux of the adage that all is within us and we are everything, including our own beloveds.

Energy is synonymous with vibration. Consequently, all our activities are a manifestation of energy. When we consciously acknowledge that another being embodies the same consciousness and energy as our being, we experience an energetic connection - a phenomenon we refer to as love.

Attaining knowledge hinges on the experience of transcendental consciousness, where we reach a state of complete rest or samadhi. This experience allows us to understand the unity of consciousness, which forms the essence of existence. Without stillness, we are restricted to experiencing only the vibrational aspects of reality, as if we exist outside ourselves. Hence, all forms of vibrations are perceived as external and distinct from our essence - consciousness - and as something that comes to us from the outside.

Upon setting a vibration, idea, or feeling into motion, it acquires an independent and autonomous existence depending on its strength. This is true of all life in nature, and it can be likened to cosmic activity. Galaxies, stars, and planets all vibrate independently, possessing their own unique characteristics that contribute to their relative autonomy. Every individual has their own unique mind vortex, which imbues them with an individualistic character.

Only when we stop vibrating like something else, when we consciously and controlled enter a state of complete rest in transcendental, absolute consciousness, and then come out of that state, can we clearly perceive the very beginning of the relative happenings of the body and mind, the beginning of all vibrations; we can see that it is about one and the same consciousness; that it becomes mind, thought, body movement, all events, and the whole world, and that there is no duality (*advaita*) between consciousness and existence, inner and outer.

When we calm the body and mind, our whole being, then we stop creating an imaginary difference between our inner essence and everything else, everything that seemed to us to be the outer world. There has never been a difference or boundary between us and the outside world, our essence and wholeness. Only then do we clearly see that the illusion we exist as separate individuals who are born, do something, and die, in itself created the illusion that there is an outer world that is not ourselves.

The illusion of our individual uniqueness creates the illusion of an external universe; the illusion of subjectivity creates the illusion of objectivity.

The outer cosmos is only as big as our illusion that we are small; how big the dream that we are special and separate from the cosmos.

All of nature and the cosmos act like a magic mirror: the more we limit ourselves, the more boundless the cosmos seems. At the moment of great awakening, when our individuality disappears, the whole universe turns upside down inside us and everything we see from the outside becomes our interior, our most intimate Self, and what we previously thought was only ours, we now recognize as everything outside. Then we literally see and experience our body and mind, all our individuality, our whole self from the outside objectively, in the best sense of the word.

When we go outside of ourselves and identify with some vibration, some thought content, then we drown in the dream of life in the world. When we calm down with our whole being, then we return to ourselves and wake up. Awakening in complete calmness of the body and mind enables a higher consciousness of the soul that exists above the body and mind and is completely independent of them.

It is equally correct to say that only the whole exists, that we are an illusion in it, and that we do not exist. Also, that the whole is indeed our essence and only we exist as reality, as the whole, and that everything exists inside us, not outside.

The awareness that we are the vibration that makes up all existence is the direct experience of the one "divine particle" that vibrates as everything that exists. If we experience it directly, then we have experienced the very divine consciousness of the absolute, because the absolute is that one particle; there is no difference between any particle and the divine absolute; that's why we use the term "divine particle" here. It should be clear by now that this "divine particle" does not actually exist as a separate particle, but is just a way of showing how one absolute vibrates as a multitude of phenomena. We can also say that all particles are divine.

If we do not consciously experience the beginning of vibration in its finest form at the very beginning of its manifestation when we come out of samadhi, then all forms of consciousness will seem like something other than consciousness itself; we will always distinguish the content of consciousness from consciousness itself, and the content will be dominant. The noise of the outside world will always be stronger than the inner silence, and we will think that only noise exists, that there is only alienation and suffering.

When we do not perceive the whole process and that our essence is always vibrating as everything that exists, then we fall into the illusion there is something else and separate outside. Then, even our essence becomes something else for us. That is a state of sleep and suffering. A state of sleep because it is all illusion; only the divine consciousness (which is ourselves) exists, and everything else is illusion. A state of suffering because it is logical we will suffer if we are not in our authentic state, who we are. If we try to be what we are not, then we hurt ourselves and nature too.

When the content of consciousness, some thought or action of the body or feeling, becomes real only for itself as such, then the insight is lost that the same consciousness is in everything, that it is all ourselves, that it is our being. It becomes something outside and alien to us. That is how the outer world alienated from ourselves is created. That is why in Buddhism it is said that the outer world - the world of form and content - has no reality in itself **outside our consciousness,** that we create the world of form (*rupa*) by identifying it with the mind (*nama*).[3] It is also said that the world of form is empty (*sunyata*), not real (*maya*). These are all different ways of saying the same thing: objects have no reality in themselves, but are real only as our absolute transcendental consciousness, whose vibrations create all forms. In reality, everything is our vibration; it is an illusion that there is anything separate from us. This also means it is an illusion that we exist as separate individuals. In wakefulness, there is neither the illusion of individuality nor the illusion of an outer world; neither is the world in us nor are we in the world. In wakefulness there is only wakefulness and nothing else. That's why there is awakening. Even the slightest hint of something "else" cancels awakening.

It is said that the world is *maya*, an illusion, but that is why it is real as *brahman*, absolute consciousness. When we do not see the world as *Brahman*, as absolute consciousness, then everything is *maya for us*, an illusion.

In other words, when we are not aware, we live in an illusion, like a dream. The dream is also used as a parable for this unconsciousness in which we spend our lives, because in the dream we hold objects that are not real as if they were real. We give them a value they don't have, **and that's why** they have an overwhelming effect on us. External reality enslaves and hurts us, but not because it is truly like that, nor because that is its nature, but only because we have forgotten our own true nature, that our essence is absolute reality, and in that forgetting we hurt ourselves. It is not the outside world that is stronger than us; it is just that we have forgotten our true nature, which

---

[3] Bhikkhu Nanananda: *The magic of the mind in Buddhist perspective: An exposition of the Kalakarama Sutta*, 1974.

is exactly that of the outside world, and we have made ourselves weak in this dream that we are living.

Therefore, we need to understand this fundamental truth: at the moment when the outer world appears as objective reality, we have already fallen into a dream, an illusion, into battle and oblivion of our essence. There cannot be an outer world separate from our essence unless we are not awake.

The realization of inner silence, and the inception of consciousness as thought and sensation within our very being, is a prerequisite for acknowledging that the creative potential of soul consciousness extends beyond the confines of our physical form and its activities. It is only when we apprehend that every thought, feeling, and bodily sensation is a product of our soul consciousness that such a realization can transcend the limits of our corporeal existence. The divine consciousness of our soul is the creative force behind all that we perceive as external phenomena, as well as all events. It is omnipresent and infinite, without boundary or exception. Thus, we come to comprehend that we are not distinct individuals, but rather we are one with the absolute. As a consequence, we "see everything in ourselves and ourselves in everything."

The material world exists solely because we impute such a quality to it. The mind is the instrument that bestows object hood up on its contents, thereby rendering them as independent entities. Thoughts attain their own reality and autonomy only when we regard them as separate from ourselves and ascribe to them a degree of independence. This applies not only to thoughts but to everything else within the cosmos. The One manifests itself in all forms, and every facet of creation is an expression of this cosmic dance. It is through this manifestation that life is made manifest, and the purpose of every event is both discerned and comprehended, including the revelation of the divine consciousness itself. The realization of our true selves, reconciliation with ourselves and the world, and attaining peace and harmony, all derive from the recognition that everything that exists is our Self and the consciousness of our soul.

THE EXACT DEFINITION OF AWAKENING AND UNCONSCIOUSNESS

We are awake when we are present in our center, when we do not vibrate outside of our center, when we are who We Are in our essence and never leave it.

We never leave our center when we know that it is everywhere, and that the limits of our being are endless.

Our center is known as *atman,* the Self, the divine spark within us, and here we use the term soul consciousness.

Since the universe is a hologram, when we are present in our center then we are in the center of the universe. Then we are at the center of reality. It is awakening.

Mindfulness is conscious existence in reality; maximum participation in reality, nothing else. **Wakefulness is not a special state of consciousness, but a conscious union with the reality of existence as it is.**

The state of being caught up in an illusion or dream is a departure from actuality, a state of existing in a fictitious reality. However, this illusory existence is itself a form of reality, for all that is conceivable is encompassed within reality's all-encompassing nature. This is why we are free to live in a state of illusion, spending our lives in existential dreams, ignorant of our true nature and the true nature of reality. Despite this, we remain within reality, akin to a fish swimming in water, though we are not conscious of it. Consciousness is participation in reality, and we may exist within it, even if we do not actively participate in it, as a child in the embrace of their mother. Nothing exists beyond the divine absolute, which alone constitutes reality. We are always encompassed by it and can never be outside of it, for we ourselves are manifestations of that reality, as is our mind. The freedom to dream up our own version of reality arises from the fact that all that exists is the highest divine reality manifesting itself in every possible form. When we awaken, we discover that every thought our mind has ever conceived is rooted in the same divine reality. Each thought is like a drop in the ocean, momentarily separate from the whole, but ultimately returning to it. The process of awakening begins when we recognize that the ocean alone constitutes the true reality, and that every drop is a facet of that reality. Ultimately, we realize that each drop is itself a complete ocean, lacking nothing and needing no return to anything, for the highest reality is ever-present.

Reality is the unity of consciousness that perceives the world and the world itself.

It becomes an illusion when divided into world and consciousness, inner and outer, material and spiritual, unimportant and important.

When we say that consciousness is existence itself, it means that everything that exists is essentially a conscious intention, an intelligent creation, a living being in a particular way: the earth we tread on, the air we breathe, the water we drink, the whole of nature, and every object is a manifestation of consciousness. Everything that happens is also a conscious creation, everything that happens to us from the outside as well as the events that we ourselves create and cause. It is all our being, because there are no limits in the conscious existence of the holographic universe.

We are unconscious, in illusion, (*maya, avidya*) when we do not see it that way but consider everything around us as dead matter, separate from us and often opposed to us.

The fallacy born of human unconsciousness is characterized by the delusion that our thoughts and bodily movements are solely our own and not a manifestation of the divine reality that permeates all existence. This profound lack of awareness compels us to commit harm against ourselves and others in the name of preserving our cherished illusions. The essence of unconsciousness is rooted in irresponsibility, which is predicated on the deceptive notion of time. This illusory construct leads us to postpone our duties and obligations for the future and to indulge in trivial pleasures in the present. Our dreams and illusions are thus founded on the false premise of time, which we exploit to justify our negative actions and our disregard for life and the cosmos. This illusion fosters a sense of separateness and specialness, leading us to perceive the outside world as inconsequential, inanimate, and irrelevant to our existence. This fallacy impels us to ignore a significant part of our being and environment, from trivial vices to disastrous conflicts and ecological crises. By rejecting the illusion of time and engaging in productive activities, we cultivate a profound sense of responsibility towards life and existence. We accept the outside world as our own, viewing it as an integral part of our reality. Through creative endeavors, we fuse our being with the cosmos, becoming intimately attuned to the present moment and the environment that surrounds us. The intelligence and insight that we acquire from creative pursuits form the bedrock of awakening.

All forms of unconsciousness stem from the erroneous belief that we are separate individuals existing within a disconnected and vast cosmos. However, this worldview is fundamentally flawed, as everything is inherently interconnected in a holographic unity. Our perceptions and attitudes act as a mirror, reflecting back to us the reality we project. If we view ourselves as small and vulnerable within an alienated and vast nature, this perception becomes our reality. Similarly, if we see ourselves as victims or slaves, we will become just that. This is because we are the conscious subject of the holographic whole and nothing exists outside of us. True awakening occurs when we realize the infinite nature of our being and break free from the self-imposed limitations of our unconsciousness. Our vulnerability and conflicts with the world are a direct result of our unawareness of our true nature. To fully awaken, we must embrace the interconnectedness of all things and recognize the power of our consciousness to shape our own reality.

THE BASIS OF CONSCIOUSNESS

Here, we must add one more important explanation, although it is difficult to understand. By saying that everything is a manifestation of consciousness, we have not reached the end, the ultimate basis of the apparent world. Consciousness is still an activity, albeit the finest, and it stands as the essential basis for every manifestation - for existence. We can say that consciousness is the essential nature of every form of manifestation in general, that everything that exists does so as a conscious intention.

There is something beyond consciousness. Behind consciousness is the one who is aware, who is awake. It is without any manifestations or attributes. It is the true source of existence in general. This is expressed in language with the smallest deviation from accuracy as "I am" or "I am that which I am".

This is how the biblical God defined His true identity. We will not promote the Bible here, but only point out that in ancient religious texts there are many grains of truth scattered, buried deeper or shallower. This biblical text is important because it directly equates the essence of the divine with existence in a unique way.

It will be difficult for many to understand (neither Judeo-Christians nor Buddhists will agree) but the Buddha expressed the same thing with the term *sunyatta*. We'll explain this a little better.

If we recognize the manifestation of the divine as consciousness - that is, if we recognize existence as consciousness itself - then the source or basis of consciousness and existence is "I am". ***"I am" is the identity of consciousness as existence and existence as consciousness in their unity.*** At the same time, there is also their differentiation, because awareness of identity is not possible without differentiation. There must be one who is aware of both existence and of consciousness itself. Accordingly, "I am" is behind consciousness and universal existence. Without "I am" there would be no experience of I (subject) or anything that is (object), **although "I am" is neither subject nor object, nor consciousness, nor existence.** It can be said that it allows subjects and objects to coexist, and for the subject to be aware of the objects.

How to practically understand "I am"? Understanding arises in that glorious silence of emptiness of *samadhi* that we experience in a paradoxical way:
- as its own essence, and as the disappearance of itself
- as the source of all existence, and as the disappearance of every form of existence.

It is this experience that connects us to existence and to reality most strongly and completely, and that also finally frees us from everything. All of this together reveals itself as "I am" within ourselves. It is in all of us, even when we are not aware of it. One can repeat that phrase and think they know what it means, but they can never be aware of its true depth, because it has no boundaries.

You yourself would not exist, nor would consciousness of your soul exist, if it were not for the one for whom it exists. Even the world itself, which is created by the consciousness of our soul, would not exist if it were not for the one for whom the world exists. That's who we are, and that's all that we are.

The fundamental nature of all that exists can be distilled down to the phrase "I am that I am." This essential self-identification as "I am" serves as the foundation for our understanding of reality. The pinnacle of human consciousness is achieved when all external distractions and objects fade away, leaving only the pure, singular essence of "I am" as the sole basis for all conceivable realities. Only those who have achieved such awakening possess the absolute certainty of their true identity. The unenlightened remain lost in their slumbering delusions, akin to those afflicted with schizophrenia. This is because, in the language of physics, the awakened or "I am that I am" is the very space in which all possible objects exist but is not in itself an object.

SPACE IS CURRENTLY CREATING EVERYTHING THAT EXISTS

According to the principles of quantum physics, the universal quantum field is the foundation upon which all manifestations in time and space rest. This field is a oneness that encompasses everything, even that which is unmanifested. While physicists generally believe that the quantum field is infinitesimally small and can only be understood through experiments with subatomic particle accelerators, ancient knowledge presents a different perspective. This knowledge speaks of the "great elements" that make up all of nature, including earth, water, fire, air, and ether or *akasha.* Esoteric teachings translate *akasha* as space, and maintain that all elements and the entirety of the manifested world arise from this space.

In the 20th century, physicists discovered that subatomic particles behave in an acausal and paradoxical manner when observed in the quantum field. They do not adhere to the logic of our world, which is bound by time and space. However, when connected into larger structures such as atoms and molecules, they behave in accordance with the laws of the physical world. This phenomenon is made possible by the nature of space itself, which is holographic and exists in a timeless present. Subatomic particles are not separate from space, but rather emerge from it instantaneously, existing in two places at once and appearing independently of linear time. This characteristic of space allows it to be seen as a fundamental aspect of all that exists.

When physicists discovered the quantum field they only discovered the true nature of space in which everything exists.

The element of ether or *akasha* is the space in which all other elements - the whole of nature - arise. That element corresponds to the quantum field. Where is that quantum field space? *He is all around us and in us. It is the space in which we exist.* The only difference is that our space is no longer pure, but has been modified into large elements, into all possible forms of the cosmos and life that exist in linear time.

However, the cosmos is not uniform, everything is possible in it, so pure space (ether) also appears in the cosmos in a smaller or larger form, breaking through the cracks of the physical universe. The celestial phenomena referred to as "black holes" are characterized by their disregard for the temporal and spatial laws that govern our three-dimensional world.[4] Within these enigmatic entities, all particles and elements arise from the pure space of the quantum field, producing matter on a spectrum

---

[4] See S. Hawking's book: Black Holes and Baby Universes and Other Essays, by Stephen W. Hawking, Bantam Book, 1993.

D. I. Mendeleev's periodic system of elements originally started with ether, all other elements were created from it. It was hidden when Mendeleev died suddenly young, as did all his collaborators. Ether was removed from Mendeleev's periodic table of elements. The original Periodic Table of Elements had zero group and zero order, where element "X" (according to Mendeleev - "Newtonium") was the earth's ether. What is now being presented in schools and universities under the name "Periodic System of D. I. Mendeljeev's Elements" is a falsification. The last time in its original form, the real Periodic Table was published in 1906 in St. Petersburg (in the textbook "Fundamentals of Chemistry", VIII edition).

Both Maxwell's equations and the Periodic Table of Elements have ether at their base - for the same reason that numbers in mathematics have zero at their base.

ranging from microscopically minute to cosmically vast. The structuring of matter in turn manifests at different scales, with smaller black holes organizing atoms and living organisms, while larger ones form galaxies, stars, and planets - all of which possess the properties of living organisms. At the core of the organization of life lies the spherical form, which arises from the toroidal field generated around every pure field. This field is responsible for the energetic aura present in all living beings, from the human body to celestial bodies.

The realization that space is singular and that the quantum field is identical to our present spatial reality unlocks a comprehensive understanding of the nature of consciousness and awareness: ***pure consciousness and awareness are themselves identical to space***. They share analogous attributes; just as space contains all objects while remaining independent of any particular one, consciousness contains all ideas about objects while remaining independent of any specific content. Consciousness can manifest as pure self-awareness, as wakefulness, or as any other thought or idea. It can be conceptualized as a finer dimension of space, in which space contains all objects and consciousness contains the significance of those objects. In essence, consciousness imbues space with sanctified life, lending existence a sense of purpose and meaning.

The "great elements" of earth, water, fire, and air, which represent the dimensions of space, comprise both our being and our reality. We are able to think because of the element of air, possess willpower and energy due to the element of fire, imagine and desire owing to the element of water, and have physical bodies because of the element of earth.

Space serves as the originator of all other elements, as photons arise from it followed by the creation of mass, which constitutes everything from subatomic particles to the cosmos.[5]

When life begins, the embryo begins to grow as its cells are constantly doubling. However, the massive increase in mass does not come from material in the mother's body; it comes from space.

All forms are actually modified space (*akasha*) itself. The first appearance in space, as its opposite, is the photon. When photons of equal size collide, they create a vortex that becomes stable, and thus mass is created. This has been experimentally proven.

In other words, space instantly creates light, and light creates matter and the entire cosmos. There are no objects that move through space, but space itself instantly transforms into objects, and thus, like a wave, it is coherently transformed by conscious intention to look like a certain object, for example our moving hand. There is no moving hand, there is only endless space, the ether, which is instantaneously and coherently created into what our senses perceive as a moving hand. **There are no objects; everything is just space that looks like a world of objects to our senses and mind.**

In essence, space is the same as consciousness because consciousness can be aware of everything just like space contains everything; that is, it becomes everything.

The concept of singular consciousness is analogous to that of space: just as there is only one space that encompasses everything, so too there is only one con-

---

[5] It has been experimentally proven that photons can behave as if they have mass and combine into molecules. Such a hybrid molecule of photons is called a *polariton*.

sciousness that pervades everything, though it manifests individually.

Self-awareness is experienced as a universal, cosmic whole that fascinates and captivates us in the same way as the exploration of outer space. Those who are drawn to the mysteries of the cosmos are essentially seeking self-knowledge, even if they are not consciously aware of it. The mind is arrested by the vastness of cosmic space, much as it is when contemplating the actions of the soul.

Cosmic space, then, is our self-awareness, our very essence, and our deepest "I am" experience. Although there have been attempts to connect the quantum field with mind or consciousness, no one has yet made the connection with space itself, with *akasha* or ether, or with human essence or soul.

We exist within the quantum field like fish in water, yet we remain unaware of this for a reason.

The Jesuits, who oversee university education and science throughout the world, have worked to prevent the unification of these concepts, a position justified by the fact that science is still largely concerned with empirical facts rather than higher dimensions. They have banished true consciousness studies from all departments, replacing it with a materialistic view of artificial intelligence. They have minimized the significance of the quantum field to the point where it is no longer comprehensible or visible, and have banned the concept of ether from science. They deny the existence of the human soul at every opportunity.

Despite these efforts, the truth remains hidden - only to be revealed when the time is right. There is no conspiracy; rather, these efforts are designed to benefit and sanctify us. If this knowledge were always apparent, we would remain unaware of it - like fish in water. Our experience of opposites is a necessary step in our awakening process.

Here, we help such awakening by acknowledging that space, ether, the quantum field, consciousness, and soul are all one and the same.

THE PHYSICS OF THE INNER AND OUTER WORLD

It is necessary to understand the action of the inner and outer world from the point of view of the laws of physics.

The basis for all physical phenomena and forms are frequencies. They are movement, and movement is energy. Therefore, energy is the basis of nature, and energy is frequency.

In his equations, James Clerk Maxwell stated how electric and magnetic fields affect matter along the entire spectrum, both scalar (non-Hertzian)–that which acts instantaneously at any point in space, and vector (Hertzian) - linear transmission from one point to another.

Following the passing of this renowned individual, scalar equations were eliminated, and only vector equations were retained due to their practicality and ease of use. However, the true reason behind the exclusion of scalar or non-Hertzian frequencies, which pertain to the physics of the ether or quantum field and serve as a source of infinite energy and instantaneous information transmission, was to keep this knowledge concealed from the public. It was believed that humanity was not mature enough to comprehend such concepts while it was still reliant on horse transportation.

The accuracy of Maxwell's prescience is exemplified in his 1846 statement that "matter may not actually exist, and that everything perceived as matter is merely a manifestation of the compression of the field." This assertion implies that objects do not exist in and of themselves but rather as an embodiment of the current manifestation of space, and that all components originate from the ether or *akasha*.

According to Max Planck, the mind acts as the foundation of matter, with the vibrations of quantum fields forming the particles we recognize as physical matter, and with our consciousness deriving from the quantum field.

Nikola Tesla's discoveries were founded on ether physics and non-Hertzian frequencies, and his patents continue to shape and advance modern civilization with many more innovations yet to be discovered. Tesla was frequently pictured with a copy of Maxwell's book, *The Scientific Papers* (edition from 1890, 607 pages), in his possession, which he read continually and regarded as a form of poetry.

Throughout history, a dichotomy has been recognized between the frequencies of the absolute (unmanifested) and relative (manifested), with similar distinctions being drawn between the visible and invisible, the earthly and heavenly, the empirical and transcendental realities. Buddhist philosopher Nagarjuna proposed that reality has two facets: absolute (*paramartha*) or transcendent (non-Hertzian), and relative (*samvrti*) or empirical (Hertzian). Absolute refers to the nature of the ether or quantum field, which can be simplified as emptiness (*sunya*) and is now described as consciousness of the present. Nagarjuna posited that although we only experience the manifested Hertzian aspect of existence, this aspect ultimately rests on the non-Hertzian aspect -ether or quantum consciousness - and that nothing exists independently. He taught that the void of the quantum field is the essence of all things and phenomena and that the ultimate realization or awakening of the self, the true nature of the Buddha, is rooted in this same quantum void.

Lao Tzu also made reference to this concept when distinguishing Tao (the non-Hertzian aspect) and Te (the Hertzian aspect), and condensed our wisdom toward recognizing the difference between these two aspects of reality within the nature of existence, as well as recognizing their connection in every action.

Here, we can label these same fundamental distinctions as the outer world and the inner world. The external would be the Hertzian or vector world that takes place in space and time. The inner world of our Self has all the properties of non-Hertzian or scalar frequencies, of eternal present or timelessness that is based on the physics of the ether or quantum field.

Some call conscious action according to the laws of the fundamental quantum field *the quantum mind.* For us, the more beautiful expression is *consciousness of the soul.*

When we are identified only with the body and its empirical mind, then we are in Hertzian frequencies and the outer world seems separate from us, opposed to us, oppressing us, and therefore we have to fight in order to survive in it. Such is the nature of the Hertzian world: we have to make an effort to overcome all obstacles in order to get from point A to point B. Individuals who share this illusion also believe they must fight amongst themselves to survive their illusionary world. Every form of effort, conflict, and violence is evidence of the operation of the Hertzian mind alienated from the whole.

Scalar frequencies are characterized by instantaneous action that transcends space and time. This is analogous to the workings of the higher mind and soul consciousness, which effortlessly chooses and manifests the parallel reality it desires. This phenomenon is known as the Law of Attraction.

Through self-realization and transcending identification with the body and mind, one can dispel the illusion of the external world. The body, mind, and world are external to the consciousness of the soul. The soul departs from the body and mind once it transcends the illusion of the world.

The human body has seven energy centers or chakras that encompass the entire spectrum of frequencies from non-Hertzian to Hertzian. These frequencies are organized into seven stages.

Humans are a combination of the unmanifested and the manifested, the visible and the invisible, the inner and the outer, the divine and the demonic. The human experience revolves around the joining and separating of these elements, ultimately leading to conscious discernment, understanding, and reunification with the divine. This is the central theme of human life and civilization.

The first three chakras bind us most strongly to the manifested world through the preservation of life energy, sexual exchange, and social interaction in order to create higher values. Over-identification with these chakras can lead to suffering and entrapment in the whirlwind of low passions, which perpetuates the illusion of the manifested world as the only true reality.

In the lowest chakras, conception of a new body takes place, a new illusion that "outside" there are "others". The energy of these centers that separate or polarize us is the most powerful: it is sexual energy. With it, we have the strongest relationship with "others" in every way, good and bad. However, in the greatest polarization, the true nature of polarization (its hidden unity) is revealed. Through the experience of birth and death we discover the nature of our own being and existence in general. Awakening in reality occurs only in relation to the contrast provided by the illusion of sleep.

When that vortex of illusion is sufficiently experienced and realized, the need to overcome it arises. Consciousness of increasing unity is represented by the higher chakras, from the fourth to the seventh. The seventh is a reflection of the consciousness of pure unity, the consciousness of self, in which there is no outer world different from consciousness itself, from consciousness of the divine soul - our essence.[6]

The mind is a place of reflection of the outer and inner world, Hertzian and non-Hertzian. All that is Hertzian is identification with the contents of the mind and the outward turning of soul consciousness through identification with the body and linear time.

The non-Hertzian quality is a turning towards the self, towards consciousness of the soul, through the termination of identification with all the contents of the mind and time. It is awakening, achieving objective awareness in the timeless present.

Everything that is low and turned downward and outward binds and enslaves us. Everything that turns us upwards and towards ourselves awakens and liberates us. It's always been that way.

---

[6] See more details about this topic in my book "Samadhi - unity of consciousness and existence".

THE CONNECTION OF THE OUTER AND THE INNER THROUGH THE HUMAN

The human body is composed of Hertzian frequencies, while consciousness is non-Hertzian. The human being is a combination of both Hertzian and non-Hertzian frequencies, the quantum field and the manifested world, spirit and matter. As a result, we have the ability to transcend time and space, to remember and create the past, present, and future, and to be aware of both the quantum field and the outer world. While externally participating in time and space with our physical body, we are independent of time and space in our spirit, leading to a feeling of eternity and timelessness. This feeling is the fundamental cause of religiosity and all cultural and spiritual aspirations. Additionally, due to human essence being independent of time and space, we can influence the manifestation of time and space.

Human consciousness (the soul) is not only independent of the body but is also identified with the body, Hertzian frequencies, linear time, and shape in space. This identification is necessary for the soul's consciousness to participate and act on both frequencies, to connect the inner and the outer, and for the body to function harmoniously and correctly in the outer world. This is also necessary for such recognition of the unity of the internal and external to occur in human beings.

Thus, humans experience both awareness and unconsciousness, illusion and reality, and all opposites in the world and within themselves, in order to transcend both states. When they recognize their essence, all divisions within and without are transcended and the semblance of an individual separated from the whole disappears.

In reality, there is only the unity of the outer and the inner, but in order to actualize awareness of that whole, it was first necessary to create the appearance that something is separate from the whole. This appearance is what causes humans to believe they are separate from everything. However, in a person who realizes the unity of the outer and the inner, the unity of the whole becomes a personal experience. Since nothing exists outside the whole, even a person's personal knowledge of the unity of the whole remains the knowledge of the whole itself. Therefore, it is no longer impersonal but is actualized as a living being, as a human who acts in harmony with themselves and the whole.

Before human cognition, the natural entity was an impersonal element. With an awakened human, it becomes a creative intelligence, a divine consciousness at work.

NATURE AWAKENS US

When one realizes the essential unity of the outer and inner world in a meditative experience, the same can be seen outside of meditation.

We have said that the key moment of awakening is distinguishing consciousness itself from the content of consciousness or mind. Practically, this means that **we recognize consciousness as existence itself** and that the contents of consciousness are only a momentary change in the state of mind, thoughts, intentions. Behind all changes in the mind stands the very awareness that enables the mind. Recognizing consciousness as existence itself, as nature, in practice acts as a great awakening and relief; all mental problems and depression are overcome in this way. They exist only as long as we continue to look at them as if they were real in themselves. When we become aware of the wider context, the very nature that makes all life possible, then we realize that all the mental contents and problems they bring are just trifles and pale shadows, actually illusions when compared to the very fact of existence, greatness, and the beauty of nature.

Our perception of the beauty of nature is based on the perception that it exists at all, and also that it is nothing; that there is being and also there is no non-being. Existence alone is enough for us. When existence itself becomes enough for us, then we are objectively aware of existence as it is.

Such awakening and relief most often occur in contact with nature, which is why we need contact with nature to free ourselves from subjective illusions. Just a little close contact with nature is enough to expand our awareness. Then we realize that we are full of bliss just because we exist in this wonderful world; that even the smallest thing in nature is miraculous. All our suffering and depression arose only because we did not see the larger whole due to narrowed attention; we did not pay attention to existence itself, to its wonder, but instead, our consciousness remained narrowed to some current content of the mind. When we are careless about life itself, it is logical that we will be depressed. In such a state, the attractive power of the contents of the mind increases, and thus a vicious circle of illusion and suffering is created.

This is solved primarily by changing the environment in which we find ourselves. Someone who is depressed does not like to stay in beautiful nature but rather in a darkened little room, isolated from natural and healthy life. By changing the circumstances and the place where we acquired the depression, we will also change our state of consciousness, the content of the mind. Then we need to change the people with whom we are in contact, who contribute to the bad state, and to look for the company of positive people who help us change with understanding. We should also take care for a healthy life and avoid bad food, as some parasites can have a decisively bad effect on our state of mind.

In the realization of Self or consciousness of the soul, the outer world disappears, or rather ceases to exist as the outer world, and immediately afterwards, the outer world is recognized as the same consciousness of the soul. When we realize our true nature, then we only see the world as it really is: as a manifestation of the divine consciousness - consciousness of the soul. Everything is one and the same consciousness that is distinguished only in illusion as internal and external, as if the forms of things and events were independent of us. When we know ourselves, we also know the world around us as ourselves. Then we see that the entire cosmos manifested itself in order for self-awareness and self-realization to take place in us. It is a rare phenomenon, but it always exists everywhere in the cosmos as a conscious subject, in a person with a soul. Such individuals always exist in the world, but they are rare. They must exist because in them the circle of the manifestation of the world closes; in them the cosmos becomes aware of itself. Without them, the cosmos would not be whole as it is, and life would be meaningless. Because of spiritual individuals, this whole world exists.[7]

When a person realizes oneself, the consciousness of their soul, the divine consciousness within oneself, then the entire evolution of the manifestation of the cosmos and life is completed and fulfilled. When two souls meet in the embrace of love, then the meaning of the existence of the entire cosmos, the evolution of life, is fulfilled in them.

These are very rare phenomena; there are many more individuals and phenomena that are only on the path to such an outcome. Much more space and time in the cosmos is occupied with pursuing such an outcome. Many more planets are desolate and lifeless. These are all

---

[7] There are also people who do not have enough soul, who act as organic portals for negative entities. Because of them, the world is also in chaos, also, it is not always only in harmony. Their consciousness is exclusively materially oriented. They are often the biggest psychopaths. These are some of the most powerful people in the world, organizers of wars, economic crises, planned epidemics... See about this game of opposites that makes up this world in my book "Religiousness: Instructions for Use".

imperfect forms of life that we can see everywhere striving for perfection, for understanding, and for the re-establishment of unity. They are filled with greater or lesser degrees of destruction, alienation, conflict, imperfection, and the absence of life and understanding. All conflicts and violence arise only as a result of suffering due to alienation from the original unity. The magnitude of evil and violence resulting from alienation shows how much individuals need the consciousness of their unity with the whole.

Life is a mirror that reflects back to us what we project into the world. There is no real separation between our inner and outer selves - they are one and the same.

LOVE AWAKENS US

All conscious beings strive to return to their original unity. This aspiration manifests in them first of all as an aspiration towards knowledge and understanding of the outer world and other beings. The indirect consequence of that aspiration is the building of civilization, science, and culture.

In contrast, direct experience of original unity occurs when we have meditative awareness of soul consciousness or Self (*atman*) in meditation. Outside of meditation, in everyday life, the moments closest to that experience are the states of pure love, kindness, and understanding that occur between conscious beings. Then, complete realization of the purpose of the divine whole takes place. In that act, it realizes the fulfillment of the ultimate meaning of its manifestation as the cosmos and life.

The original unity can be discovered in two ways, within and without, because there is no difference between our essence and the outer universe. We discover it inside in meditative calmness (*samadhi*) and outside through pure love and understanding.

When two conscious beings in loving embrace discover a renewed unity in each other, the entire cosmos experiences their joy, and in them the cosmos fulfills its purpose. We ourselves experience a fraction of that cosmic ecstasy in moments of the purest love and understanding as our own ecstasy (orgasm). Our ecstasy springs from a fundamental feeling that those moments are the most important thing for which life exists; we are ready to sacrifice everything for that state and to do miraculous deeds. We may not be aware of it, but we all live only to experience such moments; they have the greatest attractive force and provide meaning in our lives.

The basis of all suffering is a lack of love and understanding. If we are not aware and mature enough to experience such moments, to recognize them when they happen, or **to create them ourselves,** then the reaction of the mind/ego to our failure to realize the meaning of life in love and understanding is to kill ourselves and others in all possible ways. Violence has always been the mind/ego reaction to unfulfilled love and misunderstanding. Misunderstanding strengthens the mind/ego and thus creates a vicious cycle of violence.

In even the smallest event of understanding, kindness, and love, consciousness of the unity of the entire cosmos is manifested, even if you wait for a small ladybug (Coccinellidae) to fly off your hand. It is only necessary to follow their tracks to magnify these events. This ability depends on the maturity of soul consciousness (karmic maturity). Mature souls recognize and create moments of understanding and love much more easily and quickly than immature ones. Mature souls create and give love, while immature souls seek to receive it. The maturity of our soul lies in understanding that such moments of unity do not happen only as external events or with another person, although they can happen that way, but moments of bliss can also be experienced in nature and beauty. Maturity comes when we create them ourselves and make them happen to other beings **through us** - to be the bringers of the light of the divine presence.

We can train and practice to create such moments because they actually happen to us all the time, but we are not aware of them. For example, consciousness of the soul radiates most strongly through children because their body/mind/ego is young and they have not yet accumulated individual experiences that close them to objective reality and thus alienate them from it (which happens when the mind/ego matures). That is why consciousness of the soul radiates most strongly through children when their little bodies and minds calm down to relax in sleep. We can watch a child in sleep for an infinite length of time because the purest consciousness of divine soul we can see in this world radiates from their face. The more clearly we feel it for ourselves, the better we can train ourselves to enable it in our everyday life, to be responsible towards it, and to be aware of its potential, because all people were once such children. The only difference is that now they have bad dreams.

Even as we raise our children, they raise us. Children educate us in that the purity of their being spontaneously forces us to be pure ourselves, to be the best we can be, and encourages us not to make any more mistakes. We cannot raise children if we ourselves are not the way we teach them to be. Children teach us consciousness of the soul, and we teach them how to navigate the physical world. Fair trade.

The importance of this state of being unified is immeasurable, because there are vast amounts of space and time in the cosmos that are filled with incomplete attempts to achieve such realization. Countless individuals exist in an unconscious state, living in a dreamlike illusion that creates conflict and separation from nature and their true essence. To overcome this disconnection, all that is necessary is to awaken and turn towards oneself, embracing the consciousness of the soul and expressing it in every possible manner. ***Consciousness of the soul is awakened by its very manifestation.***

There is no need to attain enlightenment or become a Buddha before manifesting soul consciousness. Consciousness of the soul reveals itself through life itself. One simply needs to acknowledge and identify the natural expression of this consciousness, such as the "pearls of wisdom": tenderness, kindness, and humor; then to gradually cultivate them. This process will ultimately lead to becoming a Buddha.

By doing so, one can recognize like-minded individuals and naturally draw them towards oneself. Soulmates are always present, but the illusion of separation often prevents them from recognizing one another.

When people realize they are all soulmates, despite playing different roles in life's drama, heavenly existence on earth can be created.

AWAKENING IS NECESSARY EVEN IF EVERYTHING IS DIVINE CONSCIOUSNESS

Let us begin by recalling the nature of divine consciousness. It instantaneously transforms from its absolute state into a "divine particle" that manifests itself as all possible particles, elements, and vibrations. Thus, the absolute manifests as all life and everything that exists.

As divine consciousness forms the basis of existence and life, it also manifests into its opposite - unconsciousness and all possible states. Awakening involves the return of divine consciousness to its original absolute state.

One may wonder why it is necessary for absolute consciousness to manifest itself in its opposite and then return to its original state. After all, the divine is always what it is. The answer lies in the very nature of manifestation itself, which is an act of actualization that affirms existence. Without actualization, both consciousness and the absolute would be nothingness, which is impossible. The absolute exists even without actualization, but actualization happens only in our mind. By comprehending the actualization of the divine, we awaken and understand ourselves better.

Therefore, the story of manifestation and awakening is essential to comprehend. Without actualization or manifestation, the absolute is an impersonal and diffuse whole, and the mind is separate from it. The Absolute manifests itself through the mind as itself, but then it has a form and a body that can touch, speak, smile, and do everything else. In an awakened individual who has transcended the mind, the absolute returns to itself, but this time with the experience of all its possibilities.

In the awakened individual, the absolute is no longer impersonal but becomes personally known. They no longer need to manifest themselves. This is why awakening is numbness (*nirvana*), as testified to by the Buddha. Numbness is the most precise definition of awakening. Those who realize that the actualization and manifestation of absolute consciousness are merely illusions, and that manifestation is unnecessary, are awakened. Only unconscious individuals perceive the world as manifested, when in reality it is always the unmanifest divine absolute. Whether manifested or unmanifested, the divine absolute always remains the same. Their nature is unchanging, meaning that despite any transformations, they remain constant. One's nature becomes such that they cannot change, i.e. that in all changes, one remains what they are.

Awakening is precisely the event that puts an end to every appearance of manifestation and reveals the absolute as it is, without anything else.

Awakening actualizes the divine absolute more than anything else, more than all of nature and the cosmos. Awakening confirms that the absolute is beyond existence and unconditioned by existence.

If the awakened individual is aware that the entire cosmos is their being, then they transcend the cosmos. One who is conscious of something must be beyond that which they are conscious of. Objective awareness cannot exist in identification.

DEVELOPING A CULTURE OF RECOGNITION OF THE OUTER WORLD AS HUMAN ESSENCE

Individuals can engage in meditative practices to develop an awareness of the true nature of the unity of existence. However, this awareness can also be cultivated in various forms for all people as part of the culture of living.

There are already school subjects and textbooks that teach children about the culture of living. With a slight adjustment, using the latest knowledge from quantum physics about the connection of everything and the role of consciousness in the creation of physical reality, this knowledge can be expanded upon. It is not necessary to teach children physics as science, but rather as practical knowledge about the nature of physical reality, which proves that the entirety of nature is essentially a single conscious entity.

Before implementing such textbooks, it would need to be approved by authorities to discuss consciousness in education, because consciousness is not a subject at any university, not even at theological ones. If it is mentioned, it is always in a material context, which is absurd. The true study of consciousness is still a taboo subject in education, because some benefit from keeping people unconscious.

Children are receptive to this knowledge because they perceive everything as living beings, which is why they love toys and dolls. This is not just their imagination but their deeper and broader perception of the unity of everything. This sense of unity and consciousness fades away with age and incorrect upbringing. However, children sometimes have extrasensory perception and *siddhis*, and they easily empathize with others' suffering and react with their whole being because they perceive reality directly.

It is not necessary to take children to meditation centers to teach them this culture. They already possess it, and they need to nurture it to align with their growth and actions in the world. In this way, children will preserve awareness of their soul throughout their life and learn to act correctly in the world. Only such individuals can make the world a better place to live.

The only correct education is one that recognizes the world as a training ground for the expression of our soul consciousness. This world exists to fully develop and manifest the divine consciousness through our actions. All knowledge, culture, and science should aspire to express the consciousness of our soul in the physical world in the most correct and rich way possible. Unfortunately, the reality of the current world is far from this ideal.

People have the potential to turn the world into heaven again by discovering and following their true nature. This can start with a new education for children that nurtures consciousness instead of limiting it. The Waldorf (German: Waldorfschule) school offers a promising direction for this type of education, but it needs to be developed and become the standard worldwide.

It is a misconception to assume that religious education can fulfill this need. Institutional religions were primarily established as a tool for suppressing the awareness of the soul through mental manipulation. Within them, the divine consciousness is projected onto the authority of God, and on the Church as the mediator to God, and individuals are relegated to subordinate positions as if they were slaves. It has long been understood that those in power organized institutional religions. A religion that fails to acknowledge the divine within each person is not a religion but a deceptive system that only speaks of the divine in words, never in practice.

In ancient times, there were religious traditions that recognized the divine in everything, in every person, in all of nature. Some of them remain primitive shamanic traditions that today convey only a small part of the awareness that the whole of nature is a conscious whole and our very being. Today, their practice is mostly reduced to rituals. Mystical experiences are rare and helped by psychedelics (DMT, ayahuasca).

The correct awareness of the unity of humans and nature existed and was preserved for the longest time - until today - among the (pre-Christian) Old Believers, and the Old Slavs, especially the Serbs.

The traditions of the Serbs, even in today's Serbia, speak of the cosmic origin of people; that they are "children of heaven", that they are "heavenly people". The folklore game "kolo" directly reflects the movement of the stars and planets, the participation of humans in this movement. Lyrical and epic poetry only talks about love, but not about the love of a man and a woman, but about cosmic love for humanity. Their hymn is called "God's Justice". The oldest customs and traditions of the Serbs say that all nature is a living being and that it is divine; that the water is alive and conscious, when they come to the source to capture the water they greet it as a living person with, "Good day good water";[8] that the grain grows better if it is sung to[9]; that the sun is their elder - every

---

[8] Masaru Emoto: The Hidden Messages in Water, 2011
[9] The Music of the Plants by Silvia Buffagni Esperide Ananas. 2014

clear morning they took the children out to greet the sun, to heal themselves by looking at the sun, to receive life advice from the sun by meditative calm while looking at the sun[10]. They knew about reincarnation. Among the old Serbs, children were respected as angels on earth and lived carefree, as if in paradise. Women, namely mothers, had a crucial role in leading society.

Judeo-Christianity played a key role in brutally suppressing such old faith in all ancient peoples, opening universities, forcing them to learn basic natural laws. The reason for suppression was to force people to develop, to become active creators, with knowledge of all natural laws, and not just to enjoy direct perception like little children. So, the reason is growing up and maturing. If it weren't for such coercion, people would still be in unity with nature today, playing around the fire and enjoying looking up at the stars. Now they are developing technology with which they can fly to the stars, to touch them, to understand why nature is the way it is.

Cleve Backster: Primary Perception, Biocommunication with Plants, Living Foods, and Human Cells; Peter Tompkins and Christopher Bird: The Secret Life of Plants: a Fascinating Account of the Physical, Emotional, and Spiritual Relations Between Plants and Man.

[10] Essence of Sunyoga: Practical manual: Let the sun transform your stressful life into eternal bliss by Sunyogi Umasankar, 2022

WHY THE OUTSIDE WORLD HAS A CONDITIONING EFFECT ON US

There are multiple answers to this question. The first is simple: we empower the external world to affect us. Through our ignorance, we have created the world of objects, which influences us in this manner. The external world affects us negatively only if we are disconnected from the true nature of the objective world and unaware that it consists of the same consciousness that is our essence or soul. Consequently, we give strength to the objective world to influence us and thus provide it with a motive to reveal its true nature to us, which is the same consciousness as ourselves. ***This is how we awaken and become conscious.*** The entire objective world, life itself, fate, karma, and civilization development are all ways in which we make ourselves aware of the realization there is only one divine consciousness in everything and it is our very essence.

It is logical that the outside only affects us to the extent and in the way that we project it. The conditions of our life, work, and cultural development are all created with our consciousness. As we become more aware of ourselves and the world, the conditions of our lives become better and more perfect. Conversely, the less conscious we are of our true nature and the world, the more we project our environment as destructive.

However, the problem is much more profound. Consciousness of the soul is the most potent force that attracts people. This is the same consciousness that has created all of nature and life, which is why nature is so alluring to people. They want to live in it like in paradise and do nothing else. For individuals, harmony with nature is sufficient.

However, the divine creation of nature is only the first part of the work; the arrival of humanity is the continuation of the manifestation of the world on a higher level.

Humans build virtual theaters in nature. In these, they play all their possible roles, dramas, comedies, and tragedies. Humans consciously experience what is not visible and does not exist as natural forms in life, which is the meaning behind all events; they themselves create new possibilities in addition to natural causation, including both the creation and destruction of life. In poetry, they combine the incompatible, the mute becomes possible, the invisible becomes visible, dreams become reality - but only for a while, until they recognize everything they thought was reality is experienced as a dream.

Everything that is manifested as the world, as a multitude of objects, is connected and combined into meaning by humans, thus returning everything to the divine.

Let's say this graphically: from the One (universal field), a multitude manifests itself as a world of objects in nature; this is one half of the process of actualizing the divine; the other half takes place **and is completed through humanity** when humans reunite everything manifested, all facts and all possibilities of being, into One through understanding and meaning.

In order for people to force themselves to do all that, to experience new possibilities, they need to be exposed to challenges and struggles. If they remain satisfied only with what nature offers them, they remain unaware of their higher possibilities, which means themselves.

They would never have created Nintendo!

But neither would a rover be walking on Mars.

Even those achievements do not provide the deepest sense of why there is challenge and struggle.

Conditionality exists as a reflection of the nature of the reality of our soul in this world. Conditionality and suffering teach us most strongly the truth that we should not be attached to anything in this world because our soul is not of this world. Consciousness is primary and the world is secondary, the world is only a consequence of the projection of our soul consciousness. All the outside is our inside. That is why we can never find comfort and refuge in this outer world. And we shouldn't. That impossibility wakes us up. Death, most of all. Thus we are forced to recognize the true life of divine consciousness here and now in everything without delay. Without the experience of death, no one awakens to eternal life.

If we could find refuge in this world, we would never wake up; that is, come back to ourselves. We would remain forever attached to our projection. That is why both divine consciousness and nature itself force us with all our might to learn *tantra*: to not bind ourselves, to love freely without binding ourselves or others, to know the energy of life as basic consciousness, to consciously experience energy, to live with our whole being in order to know everything to the end, but also to transcend everything. To always be aware of ourselves in relation to everything we do.

Nature does not want us, like an immature child, to seek refuge in it. It's the other way around. Nature wants us to grow up and know ourselves so that it can find refuge in us, in the consciousness of our soul, because the soul is the creator of nature.

Only the awakened one sees that all of nature is perfectly designed to serve just one purpose: human awakening. That is the teaching *of samkhya.* The teaching of folk wisdom says it even more simply: the club came down from heaven.

HOW THE DIVISION BEGAN

All creation stems from the divine absolute, which can be thought of as an upside-down tree with its root in heaven and its trunk and largest branches in the highest dimensions. These first monads of individual consciousness are known as archangels who create all worlds, stars, and planets. As they are divided into smaller branches and individual consciousnesses, they correspond to the representation of angels who create all the details in all the worlds and all of life. Finally, each leaf represents one conscious individual being.

Divine consciousness is always one and the same, and there is a whole tree in every leaf, flower, and fruit. Our souls are the creators of everything in their original state, closer to the divine consciousness. However, when the soul is in a body, it can only act according to the limitations of that body.

In the process of branching out and manifestation, another process takes place: the process of forgetting one's essence. With each new formation, consciousness becomes distant from its source, forgetting more and more that it is all forms of existence. Each particular vibration becomes individual enough to act independently, and individuals become the beings who act most independently as microcosms.

At the end of the manifestation in the physical world, a multitude of individual forms and contents of the outer world become dominant, and forgetfulness manifests itself as a division into inner and outer. This division twists reality, and consciousness becomes a state only within the being, with external forms being held as the only real ones. Such a person is not aware of their true nature, which is the Whole as pure consciousness and existence itself.

However, there is a valid reason for this: only when concentrated in one conscious being can consciousness reach the meaning of its existence. Only in individual self-realization as "I am" does consciousness reach its universal nature and reality. In fact, in every form of existence, consciousness manifests itself as "I am" but only as a form, vibration, or thought. Only in the conscious subject does consciousness become aware of both realities: itself as pure consciousness and its unity with every form.

Thus, the loss of the true nature of divine consciousness during the manifestation of the world is necessary in order to find it again in the self-awareness of individuals. Losing self-awareness is the way the world manifests itself, and illusion is the way to know reality. In this way, there is nothing but reality.

EVERYWHERE THERE IS A COMBINATION OF OUTER AND INNER

When walking through a beautifully designed city, one can witness the fusion of the outer and inner worlds. Whether it's observing a worker constructing a building, a peasant tilling the land, or people loving and understanding each other, the connection between the outer and inner realms becomes apparent. The mere act of witnessing this unity, even in glimpses, brings pleasure and a sense of harmony. The perfection of technique is an expression of this awareness of reality, as it harmonizes both the outer and inner cosmos.

However, when there is a separation between the outer and inner worlds, destruction and conflict arise. This disconnection reflects a lack of understanding of the true nature of existence. Neglect and ugliness are the result of this unawareness.

Improvements in life are a reflection of a greater understanding of the unity between the outer and inner worlds. As our awareness of the true nature of the outer world grows, our refinement of life and environment increases. Culture and civilization flourish as we manifest our awareness of the unity between the outer and inner realms.

RELIGION IS A REFLECTION OF UNITY INNER AND OUTER

In esoteric Christianity, God becomes human through his son Jesus Christ. This means that outer space, God, manifests as the human. The human returns to their essence through resurrection, transcending the limitations of the mortal body and surrendering to the Whole, the space that is God. This is the idea of Christianity: the materialization of the soul's consciousness (embodiment) which takes place through the transcendence of matter (resurrection), and the transcendence of matter simultaneously occurs through the perfection of matter through its sanctification, through the awareness of the true nature of matter, i.e. the outer world. This is also the true purpose of the development of science and culture.

The intention behind religious teachings is to bring the Kingdom of Heaven to earth.

The hexagram symbol, also known as the Star of David, represents the unity of the inner and outer worlds. The downward-facing triangle signifies the divine consciousness descending to earth and into man, while the upward-facing triangle represents the consciousness returning to the divine. This symbol illustrates the true purpose of soul consciousness that exists in the physical world.

Buddhism expresses the unity of the outer and inner by recognizing that everything external is our true nature, or Buddha's nature, and therefore any distinction between the outer and inner disappears. Buddhism promotes non-violence, kindness, and mercy towards all forms of life and existence since everything outside is recognized as our interior, as our being. In Buddhism, the individual disappears as the source of the illusion of separation between the outer and inner world. The difference between them only exists within the human mind and ego.

The essence of religious devotion to the external God is to understand that the external is our internal. It is wrong to overlook the importance of the body and the human due to the greatness of the external manifestation of the divine. Some religious fanatics have a negative attitude towards the body and humans. Surrendering to God is challenging since we doubt if we will receive anything in return. However, we do not need to search outside for God, but within ourselves and existence itself.

Passionate devotion to God is often an attempt to avoid God. The greatest religious fanatics are those who wish to avoid God the most. Surrendering to the divine is impossible since we have nothing to surrender. Everything is divine, including our mind. It is a matter of awakening to the reality that exists here and now. When we recognize that nothing belongs to us, we have surrendered and are on the verge of awakening.

ASTROLOGY IS THE SCIENCE OF UNITY THE INNER AND OUTER WORLD

The physical body and all of its actions during life are entirely conditioned by external factors, much like a fetus in the womb of its mother. The largest external influences come from celestial bodies such as the Earth, planets, and stars, which act upon us much like a mother's body acts upon her unborn child. Upon birth, we exchange our small physical body for a much larger one comprising the Earth and the solar system, yet we remain unaware of our true nature and we lack free will. Our entire existence is a product of the functioning of the solar system, yet we mistakenly attribute our actions solely to ourselves and our physical bodies. This limited perspective creates an illusion of control, which is really the unconscious workings of the cosmos.

Our being is intricately linked with the planets of the solar system, and everything we experience and do is a manifestation of their influence. However, our perception is limited to our physical body, leading us to believe that we are the sole agents of our actions. In reality, everything is the result of the cosmos' actions, and physical bodies merely attribute these actions to themselves. This limited perspective creates an illusion of self-importance, which is the cause of much of our suffering.

Ultimately, our limited perception is a result of reducing ourselves to a small physical body and observing existence from that perspective. This narrow view creates the impression that we are the ones doing things, when in fact everything is a product of the cosmos. This mistaken view of reality causes us to act wrongly, as we fail to recognize our true nature as part of the larger whole.

A person formed by the entirety of the cosmos, from the solar system, has the apparent freedom to do what they want; however, such free will is not completely free. It is divided into two parts. The first part consists in the fact that the individual is turned inward towards themselves in order to know their individuality, but this also works to strengthen their alienation, where they separate themselves from the whole and are in conflict with nature. Then, they experience only the illusion that they have freedom and receive suffering as the end result of such freedom. The second part is when the individual uses their freedom to work on discovering their true nature, when they get to know the true nature of the outer world and how to properly relate to the world. If they progress in this, they will recognize the unity of their individuality and the whole. Such work will be supported by the whole. Taoists say that the human then has the support of heaven, to follow their Tao. Yi Jing (25 - Innocent action) says that "nothing can be done without the support of heaven"; that is, when a person is alienated, they do wrong and are in conflict with the whole, and then they do not have the support of heaven, the whole. We begin to work properly only when we work to know our higher, true nature, the wider whole that works through us, the consciousness of our soul. Then we cannot do wrong.

Every wrong action is a consequence of unconsciousness and alienation from the whole, an attempt to separate the individual from the whole, to live in the illusion that they are self-sufficient. That causes every evil action. Every good action stems from the individual's awareness that it is necessary to return to the whole, to their true nature.

There has always been talk about "liberation", but it was not clear enough what that meant. The only slavery from which a person is freed is the illusion that they exist as a separate individual who can do something of their own volition, independently of the whole. The only salvation is awakening to the realization that our essence is an unconditioned soul that as a space enables a whole that does everything within itself, together with all its apparent individuals.

In the immature stage, this return to one's own soul is explained as a "return to God". Maturity of insight is the realization that we are only returning to our true nature, and that is awakening.

We are truly born and begin to act of our own free will when we recognize our true nature, which means when we recognize the unity of the exterior and our being and the independence of our essence from both. If we are aware of both the body and the world, it means that our essence, the essence of consciousness or soul, is beyond everything. ***Only that which is independent of everything can act of its own will.***

External influences act on us only as long as we perceive them as external. The purpose of that mechanism is to make us wake up, to realize the true nature of the outer world as our own being, the unity of the inner and outer world. That mechanism is extremely simple: whenever we think of our separate "I", it hits us with something from the outside. Since everything is our being, we do it all to ourselves.

All the negative influences of the outer world that act on us arise only due to our differentiation between the inner and outer world, us and nature, when we think that we were really born and started to exist. It is only a subjective impression, but a very destructive one. We ourselves create all negativity due to the division in our mind into inner and outer. Nature is like a mirror. If we are frowning and unhappy in front of the mirror, we will wait in vain for our image in the mirror to change first. We just need to change, to "be the change we seek". All external nature will then support us automatically.

Our disconnection from ourselves is what shapes us, not external forces. Therefore, external forces do not exist.

When we recognize that the planets in our solar system are a part of us, the astrological impact of those planets on us dissipates. By understanding that Mercury represents how our mind works, we can eliminate the conditioning effect of Mercury and our mind. This applies to all other planets as well. We can observe the movement of planets in transit and experience the predicted effects, as described in astrology. This confirms that astrology operates on the principles of the holographic universe. The planet was in a particular position at the time of our birth, and when a transiting planet passes over that point, it appears as though the planet is still there.

The universe being a hologram means that the external world (cosmos) and the internal world (individual) are one and the same.

By comprehending the genuine nature of external influences, they cease to be external, and our consciousness becomes independent of any impact.

Essentially, the consciousness of our being is more powerful than both internal and external influences, allowing it to exist independently. Once the confusion surrounding the relationship between the inner and outer world, individual and whole, subsides, the consciousness of the unconditioned being emerges and is superior, acknowledging its independence from any world, whether it be the individual body or the whole that conditions the body.

The essence of consciousness remains constant within and outside us, with no multiplicity of consciousnesses. Ignorance of this true nature allows external forces to influence us. Consciousness always functions through everything that exists, so if we do not control it, it will control us. There is no neutral state.

Our only freedom while in the illusion of this world is to understand our true nature, which is independent of both the body and the whole of nature; everything else is conditional. Any other action will result in our conditioning by either our body and mind or by nature as a whole. We will only have the illusion that we are acting freely. Our actions are first taken, and then we convince ourselves that we wanted to do it "of our own free will." We only see events as random because we do not comprehend their higher connection or the conscious will behind them.

The only freedom that we humans have in this world is the freedom to know our true nature, to realize our soul, to conquer our true nature through all obstacles and illusions. In that is the whole history of the human race, all our development. By becoming aware of our true nature, we create culture.

Hence, our sole liberty lies in freeing ourselves from enslavement (although the deception can be so strong that we fail to recognize this liberty and we get entangled in a vicious cycle of our own doings). In this pursuit, we shall receive support from nature. Any action contrary to our emancipation, awakening, and advancement as a conscious being, will only ensnare us further into a greater illusion, agony, and strife with nature, the world, and others. The path of sanctification is the sole route afforded to us as humans; any other course will lead us to mire and misery. The only way to freedom is through freedom itself, which is the road less traveled. The illusion of us being distinct individuals and capable of exercising our own volition are more expansive and appealing.

Since everything except consciousness is an illusion, any endeavor other than cultivating consciousness is also illusory.

BIRTH AND DYING IS A TWIST OF THE INNER AND OUTER

Looking at a person from an external perspective, we see them conceiving a child and moving through time and space. The child grows, lives, and eventually dies, leaving behind only memories and the consequences of their actions. This is the view of a conscious observer who is observing from the outside.

However, when we view things from the consciousness of the soul, from the perspective of the objective space of the Absolute, we see that nothing else is happening other than the transformation of the divine Absolute into every particle, every form, every living being, and every event. Objective existence is continually transforming into a conscious subject, into the ego or mind of a person who observes the world from one reference point - their individual body. From this viewpoint, the body and all forms in space appear as separate objects that move in time. The person perceives themselves as an individual in space and time.

The human soul as an individual emanation of the divine whole is not born in time and space. It is only the subjective impression that arises when consciousness perceives itself from one point of view, from the perspective of the mind or ego that projects time. As a divine entity, the soul is infinite and timeless, corresponding to space itself, and eternal because it does not move through time. Only illusory entities within space - such as bodies made of space itself - seem to exist in linear time and to be born and die.

The soul, as divine consciousness, corresponds to space. That is why the soul is not born in the body, but the body is born in the soul as its idea or representation.[11]

In objective reality, the soul instantly creates a physical body within itself through imagination, narrows its consciousness into that body, and perceives from it as if it has become a separate individual moving in time and space. This is like a dream for the consciousness of the soul. For the consciousness in the individual body, it appears as a waking state, as an objective reality. This reversal is why what is night-and-darkness for the soul is day-and-light for the mind, and vice versa. The unreal becomes real.

Due to this distortion, the conscious subject perceives space from the outside as if it were separate from themselves, leading to a feeling of alienation and conflict with other individuals. The greater this sense of alienation, the more unconscious the person is of themself. However, as a person becomes more aware of themselves through scientific knowledge and spiritual culture such as meditation, they begin to realize that the outer space is actually themself. They come to "know everything in themselves and know themselves in everything."

To make this even clearer, we can imagine the objective reality or space of the divine Absolute as a ball or sphere. It has its own center point. If that sphere is con-

---

[11] This is clearly explained by the idea of the "envelope of the soul" (*kosha*) in *Advaita Vedanta*. There are five bodies that envelop the soul like onion skins: *Annamaya kosha* (food body or physical body); *Pranamaya kosha* (energy or astral body); *Manomaya kosha* (the mind that governs the physical body); *Vijñānamaya kosha* (higher intellect that brings insight) and *Anandamaya kosha* (sheath of bliss that arises based on insight into the true nature of the soul. When it is free from all sheaths, the soul is authentic and its own).

sciousness, in order for it to be current and aware of itself as a sphere, as a whole, it must always be aware of its center, the point - its opposite. Without a center it would be formless nothingness, and nothingness cannot exist. That is why existence must always have its center. It can be said that the divine consciousness constantly oscillates between itself as an absolute whole and itself as its opposite, the point or center of the sphere, the individual being or "I am" in man. That oscillation sets life energy in motion. Divine consciousness cannot only be absolute, it must also be relative, individualized. At the same time, when it is relative, it does not lose any of its absolute nature (because then it would not be absolute).

In subjective reality, from the perspective of the physical body, it seems as if one body arises and moves in time and space. It is the oblivion of existence that occurs in a conscious subject, in the consciousness limited by the physical body. Every body has its central point, the center of gravity from which the whole body receives energy for action.

The Divine Consciousness of the Absolute is infinite when viewed objectively as itself. In order to manifest in three-dimensional space, it becomes infinitely spherical. The sphere is infinitely expressed in three-dimensional space. Thus the divine consciousness becomes effective. All individual beings arise from an energy sphere that is torus-shaped. The torus has a center, the turning point of outer and inner, manifested and unmanifested.

All-that-is, the absolute consciousness of the divine, manifests itself as all-that-can-be. In order to express itself this way, the absolute consciousness of the divine is individualized into conscious monads, individual consciousnesses that are further individualized into even finer monads of individual consciousness. Like a tree, whose trunk individualizes into ever smaller branches, then into leaves, and finally into fruits that contain the seeds of the whole tree. The fruit of the whole tree of existence is the human body, and it also contains the whole tree - the whole of existence - within itself, its soul.

Since the soul is always within itself, because nothing is possible outside of the Absolute, individuation of the soul's consciousness does not occur in linear time. The soul is not reincarnated over time but manifests instantly in all possible forms, in all bodies, experiencing all possible experiences in parallel. Just as the tree bears all its fruit at once.

Consciousness, from the perspective of an individual body, appears to be born in time and space, and its incarnations appear to occur one after the other with differences due to the theme of the experiences they go through. An individual soul can also remember past lives if it raises one's consciousness a little, but if they fully awaken, they will see that nothing is happening in time and space. Rather, they will realize that they are the divine consciousness that manifests instantly and timelessly as all that can be, including every body and conscious being that has ever existed. Everything is itself the very space in which everything happens and everything that happens in space. This is the true nature of one's sanctification or awakening.

The awakened one does not perceive themselves as one who was born or does something in life; they see that the divine entity always does everything and is everything that exists and happens. They see that the mind acts like a magician who imposes an illusion on such reality, which then can be defined by the conviction "I do it." The mind imposes the conviction "I do it" on every body and on every movement the body makes. The mind does nothing but produce beliefs, and our entire life is just a collection of beliefs. We can only see this when we awaken - after life.

BETWEEN THE OUTER AND THE INNER IS WHERE THE DIMENSIONS OF NATURE ARE LOCATED

To fully comprehend how the illusion of separation between ourselves and the world is formed, we cannot simply attribute it to the mind or ego alone. Our mind is composed of the various dimensions of nature.

In ancient times, these dimensions were represented symbolically by the elements of earth, water, fire, air, and ether. Ether represents the space or quantum field in which all possibilities of existence exist. Air is the world of ideas and thoughts where all things receive their first vibrations. Fire represents the dimension where the vibrations of ideas or thoughts receive enough direction to give them the power of concrete shaping. The element of water is where the first concrete forms appear but without coherence; they can still change freely in all ways, as in the imagination. The earth element represents the physical or material world we inhabit. The world of our dreams occurs just above it in the astral - the element of water.

The forms still exist there, but they are mixed in terms of content and temporal and spatial determination. In the higher dimension, in the element of fire, form is energy itself, and energy vibrates as form. Above that, in the element of air, is the form of information, thought, or idea.

All of these dimensions collectively constitute the human being. That is why it is said that humans are a microcosm. A person can think, create and receive ideas (air), invest energy in their realization (fire), maintain their exact form in the imagination (water), and materialize them when all these previous processes are combined and realized (earth).

Ether or *akasha* is above all these dimensions. It is the space where everything occurs, or rather, the space that occurs in everything.

The dimensions of nature form a pyramidal structure, as shown in the figure.

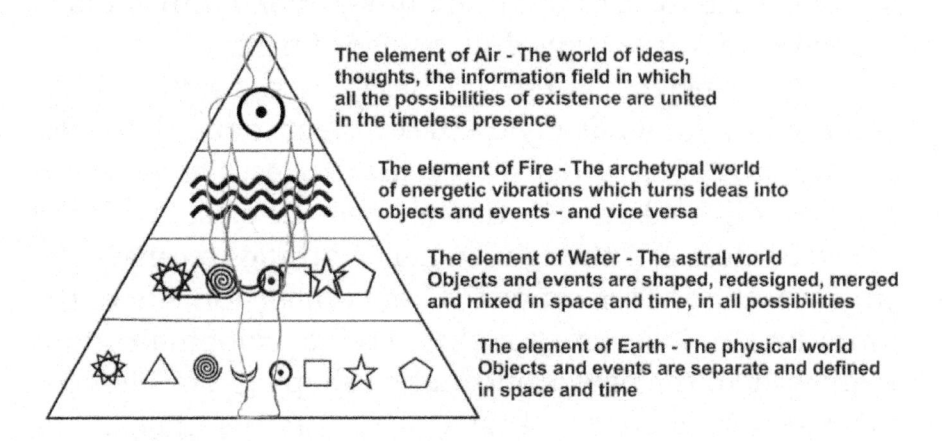

The element of Air - The world of ideas, thoughts, the information field in which all the possibilities of existence are united in the timeless presence

The element of Fire - The archetypal world of energetic vibrations which turns ideas into objects and events - and vice versa

The element of Water - The astral world Objects and events are shaped, redesigned, merged and mixed in space and time, in all possibilities

The element of Earth - The physical world Objects and events are separate and defined in space and time

The dimensions of nature act like a pyramidal crystal that refracts one sunlight into seven colors. Dimensions refract and separate the process of manifestation of the divine absolute, which is One , into many facts and phenomenon in time and space.

These dimensions give the appearance of separating the outer and the inner into the appearance of an objective cosmos, but also an appearance of reality. Thanks to them, immediacy and continuity exist side by side.

All the matter that we see around us arises instantaneously from space - the ether or quantum field. It is the one dimension of reality that belongs to the peak of the pyramidal gestalt of nature, the element of air. At the same time, there is another reality that shows us that everything we see around us was created in time and space. The house we are in was created in a certain area some time ago by the efforts of workers. Although the material from which the house is made is created instantaneously, thanks to the action of different dimensions of the nature of reality, it is re-shaped in space and time. And our physical body was created in time and space, in the element of earth, but because we also contain the element of air, we have a mind; we can be aware independently of the time and space in which the body is located, aware of the past, present, and future; close and distant.

Being is currently created from space or ether, but thanks to dimensions, it behaves such that it can act in time and space. Such behavior of being arises because of a conscious subject, because of the presence of soul consciousness in a conscious subject. All this serves the conscious subject, the awareness of all aspects of existence, which is the divine absolute. In order to succeed at this, there must be coherence of events in time and space: the physical world. All higher dimensions are summed up in the lowest - the physical world - in the earth element. Possible there is that which is not possible in higher dimensions; all possibilities of existence can be experienced in all possible aspects, in time and space, and they may be repeated as much as necessary to know and become aware of everything: that not one soul does this, but a multitude of them, so that each bears witness in a special way to the same things and phenomenon. In the highest dimension, in the ether, all possibilities of existence are currently gathered into One. In the higher dimensions, time and space are progressively compressed and disappear into One. Only on earth are we free to play with all aspects of the divine consciousness and existence as much as we wish.

That is why time and space are not just harmful illusions that "capture" us, where everything is only momentary and things do not exist if we do not look at them as some naive philosophers imagine, mixing theories of quantum physics with solipsism, but time and space are the only real conditions by which to manifest the divine consciousness in all possible ways. Only in the physical world can we suddenly become aware of all the dimensions of nature, all the aspects of existence, as well as their common meaning. In higher dimensions, we can only be aware of the nature of a particular dimension.

Only in the physical world can the divine consciousness - through the human soul - completely actualize the meaning of all its manifestations and itself. Nowhere else.

The physical world is the most concrete manifestation of divine consciousness. Only in physical reality can we touch the divine, caress its being, and enjoy all it ways, both inside and outside of ourselves.

We do this every moment; we are just not awake enough to know what we are doing.

NATURE IS ALREADY AWAKE, ONLY PEOPLE ARE SLEEPING

Awareness is the manifestation of divine consciousness through existence itself. This means that existence itself is divine consciousness or awareness. Everything exists with a conscious intention to exist in a certain way. Stones exist with the conscious intention that energy vibrate in such a way as to create the rough shape of mineral composition, the particular atomic structure that we perceive as stone. Each atomic structure represents a different conscious intention, a different experience of the existence of divine consciousness, a different vibration of the same consciousness.

Conscious intention is energy. We know that all we see as 'matter' is basically energy. In a human being, we recognize conscious intention as the will to do something at a certain moment, to invest energy in a certain way. Behind the action of energy is a conscious intention. Consciousness determines and shapes energy, strength, and will. In man, we easily recognize that the will to a certain action is actually energy, that will is energy, and that behind everything is a conscious intention. However, everything outside the human being is also the same. At the base of every form of existence is energy or will, conscious intention. We make a big mistake when we see conscious intention only in ourselves and in what we do, and see everything outside, all of nature, as only 'dead matter'. It is only about the different forms and dimensions through which consciousness acts.

At the elementary level where consciousness manifests itself through all possible forms of life and existence, consciousness is static. At that level, consciousness is static and always present, but only in a given form. A stone remains a stone. Consciousness as existence becomes dynamic in plants, where there are some basic movements and change. In the form of animals, consciousness becomes even more dynamic, but only through movement and the development of perception. Animals have perfect perception because such is in unity with consciousness and existence. Consciousness and perception do not differ in animals; perception is fully conscious in animals. Animals are simply senses that move in all possible ways. In this way, nature is always awake - in both immobile mineral form and in mobile form through plant and animal life. But all this is still elementary; consciousness in mineral form will always be only in that form, and every plant and animal species will always be as they are. They cannot change.

Contrary to that elementary level, consciousness in the human mind is dynamic, constantly changing. This is necessary for observing and changing all possible states of consciousness and all possible experiences, and for creating new ones. Human consciousness is the only one with the ability to collect experience from all other forms of life, from all other experiences, static and dynamic, and to unite them into a common sense (meaning, point).

However, due to these changes, the human mind is not always awake. Man as naturally given, with mind and ego, is the only creature that is not awake in all of nature. This is a short coming, but a necessary evil because of the great benefit given by the freedom for constant change. The mind has the freedom to constantly change its virtual reality in order to be able to summarize all possible experiences and discover their meaning.

Nature has provided all possible forms of life and existence and all possible experiences with these forms. Something completely new is happening in the human mind that nature could not provide, and that is the gathering of information about all possible forms of life and all events, and discerning their meaning. This cannot happen by itself in natural conditioning. Special conditions are required for such a thing. It takes the principle of individuality that creates the ego. Ego creates a virtual separation from unity with nature. In such a virtual isolation of the mind/ego, it is possible to freely discern the meaning of every form of existence, and all forms together, independent of time and space. No other being in the cosmos can do that except man.

This will be clearer to us if we look at it in the light of the dimensions of nature. In the element of earth, every form of divine consciousness is only a form, a certain atomic and molecular structure, and nothing else. This is the mineral world. All possible combinations of these structures are present there.

Plants are in the element of water or astral. In addition to a specific shape, they can also change, adapt to circumstances, and move a little. Plants exist as in a dream. Just as the element of water adapts to the shape of the container or the soil on which it is located, plants also adapt their shapes to the environment in order to survive. Mushrooms have an even greater ability to adapt and act. However, consciousness in the form of plants and mushrooms is just that and nothing else.

We said that the element of fire represents energy and will. It is the dimension in which divine consciousness acts as energy or force in motion. In order for movement to be correct and efficient, sensory perception must be perfect. This is the world of animals. They move and perceive in all possible ways. Also, the element of fire refers to the will or intention to do something at a given moment. And this will is perfect in animals. Each bird chooses the perfect moment to fly from the branch. He never wavers. Every cat starts and jumps at the right moment where it is intended (well, this does not apply to small kittens). However, consciousness in the form of animals is also that and nothing else; every animal species must be alike at the level of the whole species; they cannot mix - all cats are always only cats, all dogs are always only dogs. They cannot have experiences of other species and therefore cannot compare them.

The element of air is the dimension in which the time and space of all lower dimensions are condensed. It corresponds to the human mind. Practically, this means that only man can be aware of all other forms of consciousness and action: minerals, plants, and animals all together. Everything below man is aware only of its own form of action; only man is aware of all of them together. Only in the human mind is the meaning of the action of all other forms of nature realized. The ultimate insight into the meaning of the action of all forms of nature is the recognition of divine consciousness in all forms of the action of nature. It is the same in everything, but its manifestation differs according to dimensions.

If every person had only one mind and one ego, they would easily recognize their condition and wake up. The problem is that each person has a multitude of egos (I's). The multitude of I's in man is the mechanism with which man remains asleep. On the other hand, the multitude of I's is necessary for consciousness to experience all the different forms of existence. Consciousness of the mind largely collects experiences by aligning itself with the object it experiences. For this, it needs maximum flexibility. When it perceives an object, consciousness takes on a virtual reflection of that object in the mind, similar to how the sense of sight works in the eyes, when the seen form is reflected on the retina. Consciousness in the mind is virtually divided into as many parts as there are objects it perceives. That is why the mind is constantly occupied with divisions. These divisions are a state of sleep, which we can also call cultivated schizophrenia.

A split mind is both a blessing and a curse. A curse, because people feel so separated from the whole of nature, from the divine consciousness that is existence itself. Although this separation is only virtual, illusory, it makes up the largest part of the lives of average people in this world because they are identified with it, and that is why it brings suffering. But not only suffering. This situation has another side. The principle of individuation and freedom also brings a blessing, because this state enables one to gather all possible information and design all forms of existence. Conceptualizing the meaning of existence is possible only in the light of the soul's transcendental consciousness, which is a reflection of divine consciousness. Therefore, this virtual reality of mind/ego exists because of nature's connection with soul consciousness, with divine consciousness. The human mind combines the unique divine consciousness with all individual forms of existence, with nature. One is unconscious and closed in the imagination until they achieve their purpose. The mind achieves its purpose - it successfully conceives the nature of all things and phenomena - when it connects these with the transcendental consciousness of the soul, with the divine consciousness, and this connection occurs when it recognizes the divine presence and consciousness in all forms of existence.

The experience of division was necessary in order to experience the consciousness of unity. **When you consciously experience both states, you wake up.** By the way, notice that the whole of nature has always been awake, divine, conscious, but only in individual forms, static or dynamic.

Human awakening is the ability to connect all individual forms of existence into a common meaning - which is divine consciousness.

Divine consciousness is an immobile space in which everything happens through individual form and movement.

Only the awake sees that every form of existence exists because the divine consciousness itself took such a form, and that everything is divine and conscious.

Only the awake recognizes the divine consciousness of pure space as its immovable and all-pervading essence. Then, everything individually within the space disappears and only pure space remains as divine self-awareness. When we realize that infinite and unconditioned space instantly constitutes every form in space, then there can be no forms as real in themselves. They exist only in the illusion of the separation of forms and unawareness of the true nature of space.

Only unawakened people, enclosed in a separate ego, see everything else as enclosed in separate forms, as if such is not divine; as if he himself is doing something in time and space. With what consciousness we observe the world, such is the world we see.

As Heraclitus (89) said: „Everyone dreams their own dreams, only those who are awake see the same real world".

HOW TO RECOGNIZE AN AWAKENED HUMAN

If one is asleep, they cannot recognize others at all. Only those who are awake can perceive the act of sleeping.

However, strict logic does not apply in awakening. In fact, logic does not apply here at all. All individuals are in some process of awakening, and wakefulness and sleep are greatly intertwined. Understanding certain characteristics of the awakened can aid in one's own awakening. It may surprise you, but awakening is also influenced by culture and education.

A common trait among the awakened is their objective awareness of everything, regardless of circumstances. Individuals who are not awakened possess personal characteristics that define them, including their convictions, mental patterns, and habitual responses to stimuli. These psychological reactions are shaped by their individual experiences, life circumstances, and maturity.

In contrast, the awakened do not have personal characteristics that are conditioned by external factors or past events. Nevertheless, they are not impersonal; they are unique individuals. They see a unique manifestation of the divine in everything, and thus everything is valuable and important to them. They remain grounded in reality, yet retain their independence in every situation. This enables them to understand everything objectively and respect everything appropriately.

The unawakened, who cling to their personal patterns of behavior and thought, treat everything recklessly. They do not recognize the value of anything and only value what they believe in. They do not see the world as it is, but rather as they wish it to be. This is why the unawakened do not comprehend many things, why ignorance is a fundamental characteristic of the unawakened, and why internal and external conflicts arise from it.

One who is independent of the contents of the mind is awake. Day and night, individuals are forced to identify with the activities and contents of the mind. In the waking state, it is thinking; at night in sleep, it is fantasies and dreams, which can also be considered as thoughts, but in 3D execution. Thoughts and contents of the mind in the astral, where dreams occur, become three-dimensional phenomena of a dramatic character. What is in reality only a thought or an idea, a memory, is in a dream (in the astral) a living image and an event in which we participate.

The observer of all the manifestations of the mind and the world, both in waking life and in sleep, is awake and completely unattached. This is because our essence is not of this world. The characteristic of the consciousness of the soul is pure alertness and independence from any content of dreams or thoughts. It is always in its true identity, in itself, what it is, and nothing can deceive it. **The consciousness of the soul is characterized by its permanent presence in itself because it is everything**, it is always contained in everything, and therefore it cannot be deceived by anything. ***It cannot forget itself***.

When we know our true identity in the consciousness of the soul, nothing of this world can shake us or deceive us because nothing is different from the divine consciousness. For the consciousness of the soul, there is nothing that is not itself, that is not divine consciousness in itself. That is why the waking consciousness of the soul cannot be deceived by anything; there is nothing outside of it to identify with. Identification and forgetting of oneself are possible only with something else, something outside of oneself. That something different does not exist for the consciousness of the soul, and therefore it cannot be possessed by anything or deceived by anything. It always knows who it is: a reflection of the divine consciousness that is all-that-is and all-that-can-be.

This kind of alertness can be seen in the eyes of an awakened person. The awakened always sees only what is. That is why their gaze is always calm and independent of everything they see. They recognize themselves in everything they see. Asleep individuals always project their beliefs and mind contents onto everything they see from the outside. You can see in their eyes that they are dreaming even when they are awake. You can also see what they dream.

Here, on-call critics will alertly ask the logical question: why are some individuals sleeping if their essence cannot be asleep? The answer is multi-layered. First of all, individuals are also part of the consciousness of the essence and may only dream they are not. That is why the key lies in awakening and not in achieving something new or making external changes. The ability to dream is also an ability of the essence's consciousness, and this is a highly creative ability. This ability uses parallel realities, allowing individuals to be in different states, even though they are one and the same being.

Thanks to this, it is not necessary to experience all the possibilities of the manifestation of the divine absolute in physical reality or in the body. It is enough to experience many possibilities in the world of ideas, dreams, or imagination. That is why literature exists; it conveys to us the experiences of others and accelerates our growth. In fact, the more awake a person is, the less physical experience they require. The Buddha once said that an experienced horse moves even on the shadow of a whip.

There is another answer to the question of why we say that essence cannot be in oblivion when we see from our experience with individuals that it can. Not all individuals have essence consciousness. Some individuals only appear to be individuals. These are organic portals with the intelligence of the body, and they may have a strong mind that is only oriented towards the material.

They play auxiliary or important roles in the world, helping people with souls to gain experiences. These are mostly those negative experiences that people with a soul would never want to experience. The essence of the human soul is goodness, that is why it is difficult for people with a soul to experience negative states, bad things. In order to experience absolutely everything, and that means the negative, they need logistical support and help from soulless people on the physical plane and demonic entities on the non-physical plane, on the astral.

Also, due to the ability to experience all possible realities in parallel, one physical body, one person, can have different states and experiences, can have a soul and not have one, to gain and lose it, to sometimes have a higher percentage of soul consciousness in itself and sometimes less. In fact, he himself is the soul and it would be more correct to say that sometimes he rules the body more and sometimes less; when he rules the body less, then he looks as if he has "lost his soul", when he rules the body more, he manifests the consciousness of the soul more. The presence of soul consciousness is constantly oscillating, nothing is stable.

We interpret this as "falling into sin", as "the devil's temptation", but it is actually a very useful function. In this way, we get to know more quickly all possible states of consciousness and all dimensions of which we are made, all parallel realities, all possibilities of divine manifestation. Gradually becoming aware of these differences, when we have more presence of soul consciousness in the body and when less, we expand the capacity of soul consciousness that always exists in the background of everything, as existence itself. In fact, it is often necessary to lose our soul in order to find it. This is how we discover what always is, a wider whole, a higher meaning.

If we are capable of both great harm and great good, then we must transcend both. If all of these possibilities exist within us, we are far greater than any one of them. We awaken to the recognition of our true greatness.

There is only one detail that confuses us and prevents us from seeing the whole picture: the consciousness of our divine essence apparently split and incarnated in the physical world as a multitude of bodies, people separated in time and space, playing different roles, both good and evil. This is why it seems to us that some people are good while others are evil; some sleep while others wake up; some have essence while others do not. Due to our identification with the physical body and the world, it appears that essence can have different states. Lulled by our identification with different states of consciousness, we do not see the same essence consciousness in everything. We awaken when we realize definitively that the divine consciousness of our essence can experience all possible states, while never losing itself in them.

Because the soul is a reflection of the highest divine reality, an awake person who has consciousness of the soul is always correct and good; they always act readily and correctly because they always know they are not the one who acts, but are only the means of divine action. Every hesitation in action and every wrong action is an expression of the attachment of consciousness to the mind and body, limited awareness enclosed in subjective delusions. Any attachment to the mind/ego/body is the cause of ignorance and wrongful action. This was well discovered by the samurai. Before fighting, they abandoned themselves and all attachment to life, mind, and body. Only one who completely succeeded at this survived the fight. Those who have the slightest attachment to mind, body, and life lose their lives. This is also the basis of Zen.

Such awareness of the soul is also a source of inspiration for self-sacrifice. The personality of self-sacrifice, when it is objectively necessary, rests on the consciousness of the soul that recognizes itself in everything, that knows it cannot disappear, that knows the only important thing is the awakening and the work that encourages it in others who are asleep, and that knows consciousness of the soul is the only important thing in this world because the whole world rests on this consciousness of the soul.

Apparent challenges requiring sacrifice are mostly temptations created by unconscious people overwhelmed by dreams and fantasies, an illusory need to act violently and to reach their goals by force rather than achieving goals with through creativity. To awaken consciousness of the soul in themselves, unawakened individuals see meager for sacrifice. An awakened person looks at such people as little children. We cannot hate children - no matter what they do - because we clearly see the reality of their being, which is divine, and we distinguish that from their immature and changeable mind. Being is reality and mind is illusory. That is why the awakened person never descends to the level of reacting to the illusory contents of the mind, their own or anothers, and always sees the reality of being and acts accordingly. The negative activities of people who dream bad dreams cannot in any way affect the awakened person in the consciousness of their soul. They cannot even pity those people for what is happening to them, because it is impossible to pity someone who is suffering in their sleep. They cannot participate in other people's dreams as if they were real. They never descend to the level of the perpetrator of an illusory or negative act. That temptation always exists for individuals in this world. All conflicts between people arise when some identify with the contents of the illusions and dreams of others and react on the same level of consciousness with them. Those held in dreams want in every way to attract others to participate in their illusions because they feel lonely.

Only awakening is necessary, and awakening is the awareness of being. To become conscious means to wake up, to become aware of the divine presence in everything. If we are aware of a person's being, we cannot get attached to the contents of their dreams, and therefore we cannot be in conflict with them. If we remain aware of a human's being, it means that we are aware of the divine soul in them, and we then have to perceive that person as our own child, even if they are older than us and the biggest sinner.

The awakened one sees the divine soul in everyone, both in the sinner and the saint. The only difference is that the sinner looks outward from themself, toward the outside, and therefore does not see themself, while the saint looks inside themselves and recognizes themselves in everything apparently outside. None of these can actually be outside themselves, outside the consciousness of the soul. The difference is only in their world views. All the distractions of this world serve the purpose of tempting and empowering the unconscious ones.

Transcendental consciousness of the soul proves itself with the same readiness for activity as its detachment from any such activity. The awakened are just as ready to leave this world as they are to participate in it. By being ready to leave the world, they actualize their independence, the transcendental nature of the soul and its unconditionality. By fully participating in the activities of this world, the consciousness of the soul actualizes the presence of the divine consciousness in this world, in every appearance and at every moment. Everything the awakened touch, they identify as divine.

In fact, cessation of the illusionary mind divides the inner from the outer, the real from the unreal. Then, only divine reality exists and is all-that-is and all-that-can-be. Wherever the awakened turn - outward or inward, toward the world or away from the world - they see their divine nature.

There is nothing else for such a person; they see their soul in everything. That's why they always radiate grace as well as peace, enjoying the divine beauty of everything. It is only as elusive as it is present, close, and merciful. Everyone can experience it as a kindred spirit, but no one can possess it. People can understand an awakened person only to the extent they themselves understand and possess consciousness of the soul. They communicate with others by becoming the means by which others come to know themselves. They constantly encourage others by their example to realize themselves as the divine reality. Such a reality is the only one worth living. Everything else is suffering.

For the awakened one, everything is alive and aware of itself; they enjoy the rapture of love with everything that exists. It is easy to love one person with whom we are in love - to love our child or an animal that loves us too; however, it is awakening when we love our shoes with the same love, as well as the ground we tread upon, including every stone, object, or phenomenon. **We remain unconscious as long as there is something around us that we do not experience as a conscious being.** We only become aware of the earth when there is an earthquake. And then, we experience stress. The earth is aware of all of us because our bodies are its children. It also experiences stress from us because we only become aware of our body when it gets sick. We don't notice that it got sick only because we were careless and unaware of it and the world. Illness is often a way for us to become conscious, to become aware of our bodies, to return to ourselves and to free ourselves from the many stupid things that we were once overwhelmed with.

All of nature is aware of our existence. We become awake when we become as aware of our own existence as all nature is aware of ours. Awakening is actually just the alignment of our inner consciousness with the outer one, because it is one and the same consciousness; they were separate only in the illusion of our mind.

That is why awakening is the removal of such illusion; that is, the transcendence of the mind. We are slaves to our mind and its illusions only as long as we remain different from the world.

The awakened individual is conscious of their inner self, yet they perceive themselves objectively as part of the larger outer cosmos. They view their entire body and mind as just one cell in their larger cosmic body, and they control it from the outside like a skilled master. This leads to complete self-control and the ability to resist temptation.

The awakened individual sees all existence as one single being, which includes themself. They cannot be separated from themselves or others because they are everything. They are always merciful and experience everything as themself.

The awakened individual experiences their actions from both their own perspective as well as that of others, which makes them unable to be negative or violent towards others. It takes years for the unawakened to understand the nature of their actions, but the awakened has already consciously and controlled the experience that is spontaneously experienced in the afterlife.

Reality is what the aware individual perceives, and all the contents of consciousness are but dreams and suffering perceived as real life in illusion. When we recognize ourselves in everything, and when we realize that all the outside is our inside, we wake up. We are awake when we are always ourselves and within ourselves, no matter the circumstances.

The awakened individual does not separate themself from anyone or anything, and they see every person as a reflection of the highest divine reality. They participate in the illusion of life as if it were real only in order to help others wake up - when they are mature enough to do so. They do not present themselves as enlightened, rather they behave tactfully towards those who are still sleeping.

HOW THE AWAKENED PERSON SEES THE WORLD

If everything is made of the current vibration of only one single 'divine particle' (which is the same as the absolute itself), then it is the essence of our being. We are all alone; we ourselves vibrate as every phenomenon, every thing, every being, like every event, every good and every evil; as all that is right and all that is wrong; it is all the vibration of our being.

It is only thanks to this fact that we are able to correct evil and wrong, to be good; only thanks to it that we can be aware of everything, to connect the meaning of all events into a meaningful whole. In fact, we do not connect anything objectively, nor is there any need for that, because everything is already connected in One. Our sanctification only actualizes what already exists in the essence of existence.

We do everything to ourselves; everything is one being; we are all one being - all that divine consciousness does to itself through us. Such is self-knowledge.

It is because the space that makes everything possible is our essence that we experience bigger and bigger problems, why we experience the greatest ecstasy and the greatest suffering. We endure the greatest possible experiences and temptations because we are greater than everything that happens to us. We are greater than the birth and death of one body. That's why we die as easily as we season life. Just a little inattention is enough to start life and to lose it. This is simply because we are essentially much bigger than the body that is born and dies; we are the very space in which the body is born and lives and the space in which nature itself exists. We suffer because we have the capacity to bear it.

The nature of physical reality has been experimentally proven by quantum physics, demonstrating that consciousness is the basis of physical reality. For instance, the behavior of particles is dependent on the presence of a conscious subject (as shown in experiments) and the EPR experiment reveals the connection of particles in different locations. If the quantum basis of nature is such, then there is no reason why objective reality should not be the same. Our mind distinguishes between the fundamental essence of natural laws and their manifestations in everyday life, creating various theories from the essence, and conflicts with its manifestation in practice.

If consciousness is the basis of existence and the space in which everything exists, we can bear everything that exists and happens. If space can handle anything, so can we. It would be illogical for existence to show divine intelligence and for only our life to be a mistake. Our suffering must fit into the perfect logic of existence. We must recognize ourselves as the space in which everything happens, as the conscious subject to whom everything happens, in order to avoid being hurt by everything that happens.

We are in conflict with nature and life not because of nature's life, but because of our wrong attitude towards life and nature. In our illusion, we separate ourselves from our being, leading to conflict and pain. However, since we cannot truly be outside the divine reality of absolute being, which we are, our suffering is also an illusion. We dream of suffering to the same extent we dream of our life as separate from the divine whole.

When the mind is turned outward, we are aware the world is outside. When we turn the mind inward towards ourselves, we become aware that our inner being is not a separate subject in objective existence, but that the only objective existence exists and it is a conscious subject like ourselves.

HOW DO WE BECOME AWAKE WHEN THE PASSIONS ARE SO STRONG

This is the basic question posed by every clergyman. Everyone who fails to wake up falls on the question of passion. First of all, they fail to awaken because they do not have a clear concept of awakening but still cling to some contents of their mind, usually in the form of some God whom they need to know or surrender to.

If one has any content of mind they identify with, even if it looks most spiritual or divine, they will always be ruled by their lowest passions. All such is of the mind, be it the finest and most sublime or the lowest and the grossest; it is all still of the mind and belongs to the same nature. Folk wisdom says that God and the devil are brothers. Many priests prove in practice that the lowest passions go together with religiosity. In fact, passions are always stronger.

When we have the right concept of awakening, all such problems with low passions disappear together.

What lies at the root of all passions? Only the aspiration to unite with our true nature, with the whole.

The only question is at what level of consciousness we strive for union. If our consciousness is at the lowest energy center, then it will be an aspiration to experience union through intense action that exchanges energy with nature and other beings. This may manifest as extreme sports, challenges, or intense physical activity. If our consciousness is at the level of the second energy center, then we experience union through the exchange of energy with another being, through intimacy. If our consciousness is at the level of the third energy center, we experience the union and realization of our energy and being through affirmation in society - through family, public involvement, and work. Only from the fourth (heart) energy center upwards do we experience the realization of our deepest aspirations from within a wider whole. Only in the seventh energy center is there no outside object with which we strive for union; there, the absolute is recognized as itself in everything, and individuals reach self-knowledge and permanent awakening.

Therefore, the problem is not the passions themselves, but the level of consciousness with which we act and experience the world. If we are at a lower level of consciousness, the world of objects has a stronger and more convincing effect on us. We feel the need to have a stronger effect on objects, and according to the mirror principle, they then have a stronger effect on us. That is why those who operate through the first chakra fight so fiercely with themselves, with life, and with others. The better we understand the true nature of the world of objects as our being, the less that world has a conditioning effect upon us.

In essence, every passion is driven by the desire to unite with the whole - our true nature. It is only a question of the level of consciousness as to how we will express passion, whether naively and immaturely through objects and lower senses, or in the right way through intellect and spirit.

Each level of consciousness has its own logic. When we are at the lowest level, then for us the world of separate and alienated objects has full reality. We think we have to act on objects in order to achieve results, that the stronger we act the better the results will be. We only worry about consequences when we have to. However, in the holographic universe, everything has a price; we face absolutely all consequences. Only the cheese in the mousetrap is free - and the sweetest.

Since all growth contains an aspiration towards union with our true nature - the whole - in whatever state of consciousness one expresses themself, they can play a positive role; they can bring experience that will bring others closer to awareness of the whole - our true nature. And indeed, for many spiritual people who have realized their passions, they have been the real fuel for ascension. They were like the carrot on a stick that prompts a donkey to move forward (in esoteric teachings, the donkey is the symbol of the mind/ego and the base passions; Christ enters Jerusalem, a symbol of the Self, riding on a donkey: he has mastered the body and the mind/ego).

When we are in alignment with our true nature, we no longer have desires or passions because we realize that everything we seek is already within us. However, when we are disconnected from ourselves, we crave the experience of possessing everything and we passionately strive to return to our whole self. Our desires and passions are actually a naive expression of our longing for our true nature projected onto external objects.

Interestingly, those who have never faced their passions will never awaken to their true nature. Passions are experiences of opposites that force us to awaken. As long as we are content to sleep, we have no motivation to wake up. Nothing from this world can convince you that the reality you experience upon waking up is incomparably more beautiful and richer than even the most beautiful dream. Sometimes it is necessary to break from a dream roughly in order to awaken, and passions can serve as the experience opposite to awakening. Passion is the opposite of awakening, but at the peak of passion and the ecstasy it brings, we catch a glimpse of the other side –that of peace and fulfillment. The orgasm experienced in union with another being is just a small taste of the bliss of union with the whole. Passions are not inherently bad, but they are attractive because they lead to the same goal as awakening. In turn, we must be fully prepared to deal with the consequences of our actions when we fulfill such passions.

The one who can stop them at any moment has transcended his passions, not the one who has numbed his mind and body so that he does not experience passions. We overcome passions by training ourselves to stop them when they are at their peak, not by avoiding them so that we don't have them at all. In order to be able to stop the rapture of passions when they are at their strongest, it is necessary to understand the true nature of passion and oneself. When we see perfectly clearly the essence of passions, what their meaning is, then we automatically get rid of them. Then they will not appear in the future. If they come back, it only means that we did not understand them perfectly.

AWAKENING IS BEYOND TIME AND SPACE

We are both the one who vibrates (subject) and what is shaped by our vibration (object). We need to establish this awareness of the unity of the inner and outer forever, in every moment of our lives. What separates existence into inner and outer worlds is time. Time is the way we forget ourselves, our timeless essence. Time is a dream that we are separated from the whole, that we are not the whole but a small subject within it. ***Time is essentially just our postponement of awakening to a timeless reality. This means that we constantly postpone the constant presence of self-awareness in every moment and in every action.***

The awareness that we are both a subject that is aware and an object that we are aware of must be constantly present to us in every action in every present moment. This is the practice of *vipassana* and *satipatthana* in Buddhist meditation.

If we do not recognize our being in everything we see and experience from the outside, then it will be difficult for us to maintain self-awareness. On the other hand, only when we always have a pure awareness of ourselves independent of time and action can we recognize our being in everything outside. The exterior and interior of our being come together only in the reality of the present moment because they were never separate to begin with. As long as we postpone the time when we become aware of ourselves as the pure existence of all that exists in the present moment, we create the illusion of separation between the outer and interior world of our being.

When a Buddhist monk practices present-moment awareness in his whole being (*vipassana*), he interrupts the time in which he postpones this act of present moment awareness. **Time is the postponement of self-awareness.** In fact, all our lives in this world consist of a great postponement of self-awareness in all possible ways, of infatuation with all possible nonsense. Self-awareness causes the monk to disappear as a separate subject, and only the objective whole remains, which is also a conscious subject.

To be aware of oneself is to be aware of oneself as a whole. That is why the paradox occurs that only when we disappear as an individual, when we are not identified with body and mind, then we become more ourselves, closer to ourselves, and we experience the greater bliss that we do not distinguish from self-awareness and existence itself. The transcendence of body and mind strongly attracts us when we are spiritually mature. This is because in transcendence we become objectively aware of ourselves as the space in which everything else exists. When we transcend ourselves (as body and personality) we become greater than ourselves, and therefore more fulfilled by ourselves. Our consciousness has become suitable for space (according to Hui Neng and *Mahamudra*) because it is capable of knowing everything else. Consciousness is capable of knowing everything else, every object, because it is essentially every object.

Consciousness is space itself.

When we are not aware of the true nature of space, when we do not see that everything is made of space, then we are remain unaware; we react incorrectly and act towards objects that are actually made of space. If objects were different from consciousness, we would never be able to know them. Enlightenment always happens in the moment as an awakening.

Time and space that separate everything exist only as a lack of self-awareness here and now. Consciousness always recognizes itself in everything.

The moment of awakening does not really exist. There will never be that moment that you remember as the beginning of awakening.

Existence is our beginning; consciousness is existence; alertness is conscious existence. Awakening is in such unity with existence that it cannot be said awakening begins at one moment and was not there before, but only that unconsciousness disappears and the awakened one remains what they always were (like existence itself that always exists).

Awakening is similar to experiencing the death of a loved one. Only then do we become aware of what the other meant to us, how much we loved them, how much we failed to express all our love and gratitude to them. We become aware of every offense against them. We needed their disappearance to become aware of it. Losing a loved one made us aware of the true nature of their existence. Then, we realize we have to make both love and the true nature of existence conscious while those we love still exist; to increase awareness of the presence of the soul here and now, and not only when we experience loss. We must not be careless towards existence in any moment, nor towards our neighbors. It is always easy to be careless and unaware because existence always supports us in everything we do, gives us all life, carries us like a mother carries a sleeping child.

Love and attention to your neighbors, to all living beings, to every form that exists, are the means of the fastest awakening.

AWAKENING HAPPENS IN TIME AND SPACE

If the fundamental basis of nature is the quantum field, which shows and proves that in the micro world everything is in unity beyond space and time, then why do we believe that the macro world we live in is different? It is the same everywhere, there is no boundary between the micro and macro world where unity ends and separation begins. Such a border does not exist except in our mind as fiction and belief. These fictitious borders are the foundations of our unconsciousness - illusion.

In our dream state, we believe that the quantum field is a minuscule entity only accessible through experimenting with elementary particles in large accelerators. However, this belief is just an illusion that scientists are particularly susceptible to. The quantum field, also known as ether, was defined as *akasha* in ancient times by the science of samkhya.

Maxwell's equations of the electromagnetic field and Mendeleev's periodic system of elements were based on the concept of ether. However, at the beginning of the twentieth century, the concept of ether was banished as a basic principle from physics and biology.

Akasha, meaning space, is the most general and attributeless element that contains everything else with any properties. This is just another way to describe the quantum field. Hence, the quantum field is the cosmic space in which the whole of nature exists. We observe it all day long, but we only see the contents within it, not its true nature as a quantum field. Our consciousness is always focused on some content within space, causing us to overlook the true nature of consciousness itself. We are missing the true application of gestalt therapy, which can be illustrated by a simple example where a teacher draws a dot on a blackboard and the students says they see the dot and no one pays attention to the board, to the broader basis or context that enables what they see. Similarly, we are first and foremost the space itself, then any content in it, such as the mind, body, spouse, children, finances, etc. Although we are all content, we are primarily the space, because **all content is a modification of the space itself**. Nothing exists separately and by itself, which is why everything's true nature is emptiness or space, ether or *akasha*.

When we see everything's true nature as a modification of the whole or space, we are awakened. When our consciousness is narrowed down to a particular shape or content in space, we are dreaming. That's all that happens.

Space or the quantum field is divided so that we can distinguish between Hertzian (vector) and non-Hertzian (scalar) stationary being. Hertzian or vector is the external world in time and space that we perceive with our senses in linear time. Non-Hertzian or stationary being is what we perceive with our mind as our inner essence, the eternal or timeless present. In meditation, we directly experience the non-Hertzian state by calming the body and mind, enabling us to experience eternity within ourselves. Every movement of the body and mind belongs to the vector or Hertzian being in time and space.

Although it is all one and the same, all space and exterior gathered into a unity that we experience as our interior or essence is how our essence is always available. If there were no division into outer and inner, non-Hertzian and Hertzian, our essence would never be available here and now for self-awareness. This apparent dualism is necessary for the awareness of ourselves and the world. Self-awareness and world awareness are mutual, as described in the ancient science of samkhya, where *purusha* represents the inner, timeless, stationary essence of man, and *prakrti* is nature, all external vector movement, including the mind.

The nature of the outer world is not only reflected in the rough forms that we see in nature, but also in all the psychodrama that we experience through events. The Absolute is all-that-is manifesting as all-that-can-be. Individuals are conscious subjects of this manifestation, and non-Hertzian and Hertzian aspects intersect within them, enabling awareness of both. Individuals are made up of both aspects in order to realize them. Once one becomes aware of an event or phenomenon, a fact, a relationship, or a meaning, it is never repeated in the same form. While things may repeat themselves and people may become stuck in a situation, this occurs only when they do not accept that everything is happening for their sanctification and because of them. In other words, until they see all nature as their being. When someone becomes conscious of something, that consciousness returns to the Absolute as self-consciousness, and life continues on to higher forms of existence. If individuals do not come to consciousness properly, then things are repeated as much as necessary to bring them to consciousness properly.

Individuals are conscious subjects through which the manifestation of all-that-is and all-that-can-be becomes conscious. That's why individuals do and try everything they can, without limits, including all possible opposites, both what they should and should not do.

The older and more mature an individual soul is in this world, the more capacity it has to withstand greater opposition, suffering, and stronger experiences. When observing someone experiencing great suffering and events, gladly sacrificing even their life to fulfill them in a just way, do not feel sorry for them but admire them for their capacity to do so. Of course, this balance between opportunity and event is not always ideal. What is beyond the realm of endurance is sometimes experienced. That's when suffering becomes overwhelming and where help is needed for an individual to overcome their difficulties. Although suffering is a discrepancy between possibilities and circumstances, suffering is also an incentive for individuals to expand their capacities and understanding and to be present in their consciousness. Therefore, suffering can be a great teacher that aids in development. We can compare suffering to the calluses on the hands of a hard worker. If they were not of value, the worker would not have them.

KINDNESS HARMONIZES THE OUTER AND INNER WORLDS

In order to harmonize the inner and outer world in our experience, to realize complete unity, no philosophy or science is needed. Whenever we do something right and well, we harmonize the outer and inner world. The illusion of the separation of our essence from the world has been the cause of every wrong thing we have ever done. Every righteous act is an alignment of our essence with the whole, an act of awakening. Being awake just means being correct, good, positive, and aware of the whole as oneself.

Every act of love and kindness is a way of integrating our essence with the divine or cosmic whole, with reality. Our actions are divided according to the dimensions of which we and the entirety of nature are made.

All physical work and effort connects us with the whole. When we work correctly and usefully for the benefit of all, it elevates our consciousness in the whole. However, when we work destructively, there is no ascension. This corresponds to the element of earth.

Every feeling and imagining that expands our capacity for compassion, insight, and experience also connects us to the whole. If our feelings are selfish, fear-filled, or lack empathy, then there is no ascent towards unity and we remain separate. This corresponds to the element of water.

When our impulses, will, and the intentions with which we direct our energy are always conscious, we discover that such conscious acts of will and energy unite us with the whole. However, when such are spontaneous and unconscious, then there is no elevation and we remain separated and alienated. This corresponds to the element of fire.

When we think correctly and in accordance with our actions and circumstances, when our minds are filled with empathy and conscious energy, and when our minds are open, we open ourselves to the whole. This corresponds to the element of air.

When our thoughts, words, feelings, and actions are aligned and act as one unit, we rise to the divine. We recognize the divine in the present moment, here and now. This corresponds to the element of ether. Whenever we are divided in our being, thinking one thing, doing another, and feeling a third, we act wrongly, leading to the illusion of separation and to conflict with both the whole and ourselves.

Since we are a whole, conflict with something or someone outside is always directly related to (and even caused by) the conflict within ourselves.

The joy and elation that we experience when we do something good, when we help someone, when we improve life in any way or develop culture and civilization, proves that we rise to higher dimensions of existence, unite all dimensions of existence, become whole, and harmonize with the whole.

In fact, there is no other reason to do right in everything and be good to others than because there are no "others." All that exists is ourselves, and we must act accordingly.

MEDITATION IS A DIRECT COMBINATION OF INNER AND OUTER

Through the practice of meditation, we can align ourselves with all the dimensions of the outer cosmos by becoming aware of all the dimensions of our being. This involves being aware of our whole body, all feelings, expressions of will or intention, and our mind. Various forms of meditation, such as Buddhist meditation and zazen, emphasize this practice of mindful awareness.

There is no other way to directly recognize the unity of the external and the internal.

Meditation is essentially the practice of stillness. When we are completely still with our entire being, we can experience sanctification. This stillness helps us stop identifying with the contents of our mind and to perceive the outside world as separate from us. This leads to an awakening of consciousness and an awareness that consciousness is existence itself.

Wakefulness is not a state of consciousness, but existence itself. The disturbances and agitations of our mind only hinder us from experiencing this reality.

By calming down and being still, we simply exist and become aware that consciousness and existence are not separate. We realize that we are that consciousness and existence, and that the whole is our essence. When our mind is calm, we can see the true essence of our being and the outer cosmos. In meditative calmness, we experience ourselves and our essence more strongly than ever before, even though we disappear as individuals. Through the practice of meditation, we can directly recognize the unity of the outer and inner dimensions of our being.

THE DEVELOPMENT OF SCIENCE AND CULTURE IS AN INDIRECT CONNECTION OF INNER AND OUTER

Everything that has ever been done in this world, every act of improving and perfecting life, understanding the world and ourselves, has been an acknowledgement of the unity of the outer and the inner. This has been the work of our collective awakening.

Every destructive and negative action we have ever taken has been a result of the illusion of separation between our essence and the outside world. This illusion has caused a life of conflict and suffering.

Understanding ourselves and the world around us is essential for our well-being and fulfillment. However, in practice, we have yet to achieve this prosperity. Until now, people have been taught that they are separate from the outer world, that they are sinful, and that God is distant from them. This has led to the creation of a world that is alienated, sinful, and devoid of God, based on beliefs about separation and sinfulness.

Major cities are often a good imitation of hell. Shanghai, New York, Dhaka, Mumbai are prime examples of inhumanity. People are still at war with each other, viewing each other as alienated and opposing objects. Ignorance drives them to destroy nature. We live in a civilization built on ignorance, alienation, injustice, and conflict. Nevertheless, we should not be discouraged and believe that a better world cannot be built in the future. People who make mistakes should be seen as immature children who grow and learn over time. All the saints remind us that a better world is possible, that the divine world is already here, and that we simply need to recognize it and wake up.

Hints that people are unified with the world have always existed in the form of mysticism - the oldest spiritual tradition. However, institutional religions have created a separation between people and the divine by claiming to unite them. This claim is false, as there has never been any separation between people and God. What can never be separated cannot be joined. Religions have always tried to fix what isn't broken. They have based their institutions on mediating between "sinful" people and God. It has always been more important for them to portray people as sinful than to reveal the true nature of the divine. That is why they most vehemently condemned any identification of people with the divine.

The only heaven is awakening. The only hell is the unconsciousness of an unawakened person.

Currently, science does not recognize the soul at all. It works only with material facts and objects. Although this approach has been necessary until now, it is the lowest level of scientific development. If we can survive waiting for science to understand the true nature of the conscious subject participating in a scientific experiment, the world will become a much better place to live.

The only true recognition of the primordial unity of the inner and the outer is possible through a conscious understanding of all dimensions of existence. This requires a scientific approach. A science of self-knowledge was established a long time ago as yoga, a discipline of meditation, the basic principles of which were recorded by Patanjali.

The same process expressed externally through collective development takes place through the natural and social sciences. The development of science and technology in general is actually the development of the application of soul consciousness with greater precision and on a collective level.

Our true being is nature itself. Science is the knowledge of the laws of nature. We cannot otherwise fully manifest the consciousness of our soul if we do not understand all the laws of nature with scientific precision.

We have to start with ourselves; that is the practice of meditation. Only in this way will scientific insight into the entirety of nature be correct. Meditation is the basis of every future culture and the very survival of man. We cannot do anything good and positive in the world if we forget ourselves and deal only with the 'outer world' because that 'outer world' is also ourselves and we are not aware of it. This is how we come into conflict with ourselves and the world. Everything is connected because there are no boundaries between inner and outer, small and big. Everything that is negative in this world is done by people who are not meditators. In other words, who are not aware of themselves and therefore cannot be aware of the true nature of the outer world either. They have built a modern civilization that is largely inhumane, that destroys and pollutes nature.

We are comforted by the fact that we are still in the initial, developmental phase of the true civilization we are talking about here, one based on the consciousness of unity. Hence the need for books such as this that talk about awakening. In a few thousand years, we will see positive results.

WE RULE THE OUTER WORLD ONLY AS MUCH WE RULE OURSELVES

The outer and inner worlds are intertwined and cannot be separated. We are conscious subjects of the outer world, and therefore, it is an extension of ourselves.

However, we perceive it only through the sensory organs of our body. Our actions in the world are only as correct as our understanding of ourselves, and vice versa. To react correctly to the events of the outer world, we must understand the connection between the inner and outer worlds.

To master the energy of the outer world, we must first master the energy within ourselves. When we realize that the inner and outer worlds are one and the same, we become free from external influences, and the conscious subject becomes independent. The conditioning effect of the outer world on us works only to the extent that we are isolated and separated from it, making ourselves powerless. Conflict with the world is primarily our conflict with ourselves, and the first condition for understanding and arranging the world is to understand ourselves.

Divine Consciousness supports each individual form to be as it imagines itself to be. If we see ourselves as small and powerless slaves in conflict with the world, that is what we will become.

HERE'S THE GOOD NEWS:
WE CAN NEVER BE AT A LOSS

If we accept the notion that the universe is a hologram and that our essence or soul is the universe itself, unbound by time and space, then this is incredibly encouraging news. It implies that nothing we encounter during our lives is ever lost or less valuable than anything else. Every experience holds the same value and is encompassed in the timeless universal field.

The fear of death and loss arises only from the illusion that we are small, isolated individuals fighting for survival on our own.

To elaborate further, the foundation of everything that exists is the universal quantum field, also referred to as the *akasha* or ether. Its finest vibrations act like subatomic particles, with differing vibrations resulting in different actions, atoms, and elements. All distinctions in the components of nature are based on distinct energy vibrations from the same universal quantum field demonstrating conscious intention.

This conscious intention is manifested in all possible forms, with every element and form in nature existing with the conscious intention of being what it is in every moment. However, it is insufficient to manifest in simple forms. Conscious intention also created a conscious subject, the human being, who not only experiences all possible forms but also creates new possibilities.

The consciousness of the human mind is the same consciousness that manifests all possibilities of the universal field, but personalized to a specific action in time and space. The human mind triggers specific possibilities from the universal field and thus brings them to fruition in time and space. However, humans never do anything new - they only activate certain possibilities from the universal field in which all possibilities already exist. Through the human mind, the implicit universe becomes explicit, and the inner and outer world, the micro and macro world, the implicit and explicit order come together (but also separate) in the human mind.

However, this should not be understood as fatalism. Humans extract certain possibilities from the timeless universal field, which through their actions are manifested in time and space, and with this they do three things, which can be compared to the *gunas* from the Samkhya theory:

First, they help actualize all possibilities of the divine to manifest. Without their actions, these possibilities would not have manifested. (Guna *tamas*: causation and conditioning.)

Second, they test everything manifested in order to connect the manifestation of everything, everything "they did" and what they didn't, and what they should have done, and to understand what "nature itself did." (Guna *rajas*, action, testing all possibilities and opposites.)

Third, they create new combinations and possibilities from the manifested. (Guna *sattva*: synthesis into a higher sense.) Although the universal field contains all possibilities, they are unlimited. Creating new possibilities is the essential role of the conscious subject, humans. It is precisely the freedom to create something new that confirms the very unconditionality and limitlessness of the universal field, the unconditionality of the divine consciousness that makes everything possible. It gives freedom of existence to everything, to all possibilities, and to those that are shown to be constructive and destructive, to all opposites.

Creating new combinations and possibilities opens up space for everything new and unknown, and that is exactly what gives life to everything. Precisely because it is transcendental and unconditioned, the divine comes not only through all that exists, but also through all that is new and unpredictable. Key discoveries and the solutions to many of our problems came precisely through something completely unforeseen. The new and unexpected gives both insecurity and joy in life. There is no such thing in a predictable system that only seeks security.

This third is the least present. It is creative action. The first two actions, conditioned by causality, are much more present when a person acts conditionally and falsely attributes to themselves "free will" and "power of action". Most people live in that illusion. Those who are truly creative see the illusion, but they also see that there is freedom of action, *that it rests on knowing the meaning, on the responsibility to connect the meaning of each action with the holographic whole to which it belongs, on recognizing the whole in every action, on recognizing the essential role of oneself as a conscious subject in that recognition and connection.* That is human creativity.

Any creativity that does not connect the conscious subject with the whole of existence in kindness and understanding is destructive creativity. And such is possible in the freedom to express everything that can be expressed. Such destructive creativity always originates from the limited mind in humans, or from the artificial intelligence such a limited mind has created. Positive creativity that connects everything to the whole can only come from the consciousness of the transcendental being - because it comes from the whole itself.

In the freedom of everything to be as it is, there can also be someone who harms others to save themselves, who fights against others to "succeed" in something. Thus, in the end, they always destroy themselves (although with closer observation, they can notice this destruction in themselves already at the beginning). A wise person perceives that in all others there is the same consciousness that enables themselves, that everything is made of the same substance of the whole, and they try all possibilities without destruction; by recognizing the connection of everything, they accelerate their enlightenment and awakening.

Humans thus become aware of the nature of the whole as unlimited, which means unconditioned. Thus they become aware of their true nature, their essence, as unconditioned and unlimited. Through their free actions, the divine entity manifests its awareness of its unconditionality, its limitlessness. Humans are only conscious subjects.

Every action has its result, every action a reaction, because everything belongs to one universal field. Every work and every phenomenon always belongs to the whole, which is a hologram. The universal field is a hologram, and every phenomenon is only its small reflection, inseparable from the whole.

Connecting all action into meaning, understanding the nature of action, gives vitality and meaning to our lives. It fills us with satisfaction. Our lives are meaningless and painful only to the extent that we do not connect the nature of our actions into meaning; that is, to the extent that we act wrongly. Wrong action exists, and it is action that does not take into account the consequences, that does not see the causes, the logical connection of cause and effect, that has the illusion of being separated from the whole, that does not see that everything is a holographic divine whole, that does not see that the perpetrator is in unity with all that is committed, that each subject is in fundamental unity with all objects. Destructive action and violence always occur as a consequence of such ignorance. And such non-recognition and destructive action is one possibility in the universal field.

Negativity repeats itself to us only because we have not realized the meaning of its occurrence. The only evil is ignorance, preventing a person from learning. The loss of one's life is only the loss of the opportunity to learn and become aware of all experiences, and that is why it is a great and painful loss. However, it is painful only from the point of view of the body and mind, because even after death experiences and learning continue.

Every good action is a conscious or unconscious connection of individuals with the whole. Therefore, kindness is always a fundamental indication of soul consciousness, working without any particular pattern or logical consequence. True goodness is unconditional, self-sufficient, and serves as its own purpose because it belongs to the consciousness of the whole. Through kindness, consciousness of the whole works on us like a caretaker looking after their child. People with maternal instincts are intuitively aware of this nature of the whole, which is why a mother's love extends beyond their own child, spreading spontaneously to all beings and the entirety of existence.

Through their actions, individuals test all possibilities and bring them into meaning, recognizing them as holograms and consciously connecting them with the divine whole. More precisely, the divine entity consciously manifests itself through individuals.

By connecting each part with the holographic whole and understanding the consequences of all actions, individuals experience karma as karmic maturation. As the individual soul of a person matures karmically, it becomes aware of the divine whole as a hologram. Until then, it perceives very little of the causation of a "higher force" and has limited perception, thinking that it acts alone or that things happen by chance.

When an individual soul reaches full maturity and becomes aware of its divine nature, it discovers that it is a holographic entity that manifests all possibilities and actualizes them through all possible activities and forms. At this point, it stops distinguishing between its interiority, individuality, and the outside world or existence itself. The individual itself is the meaning of all events and phenomena.

Therefore, every action and experience has equal divine value if the meaning of the experience is sanctified. Every action an individual takes only serves to make them more conscious and actualized, allowing them to return to the divine whole as a conscious experience of itself. As a result, human experiences cannot disappear even after the disappearance of the human body, but through individuals, these experiences always become more complete and realized.

DREAM OR REALITY - HUMAN OR BUTTERFLY

Let's recall the famous story of Chuang Tzu in which he briefly says: I dreamed that I was a butterfly, that I was flying from flower to flower. The dream was so real that when I woke up I didn't know if I was a man who dreamed he was a butterfly or if I was now a butterfly dreaming he was a man.

Many interpreters use this story to show how physical reality is an illusion. That is wrong. In fact, through this story, Chuang Tzu expressed the view that everything is one and the same reality, both the world of dreams within us and the physical world outside of reality. It is our mind that makes the differences between them and that is the only illusion. Chuang Tzu wanted to say that the outside world and our inside are one and the same thing.

In waking life we can be in an illusion as great as if we were in a dream. In a dream, we can be as awake as if we were awake (lucid dream, astral projection). It is only the way of looking or the attitude of the mind, the underlying conviction, that makes the difference. Objectively there is no difference, it is all one and the same existence.

The same insight is found in the saying of *Advaita Vedanta* that the outer world is an illusion if viewed only as the outer world, but it is reality if viewed as *Brahman*, as the absolute consciousness that we ourselves are.

IN OUT-OF-BODY EXPERIENCES, WE DO NOT LEAVE OURSELVES

Speaking about the unity of the outer and inner world, we cannot avoid the topic of out-of-body experiences.

But beyond those abstract explanations, we can say that the more clearly a person maintains their awareness of themselves outside of the physical body, the more they perceive that state as a greater proximity to themselves, to their essence, as a greater revelation of themselves, greater bliss in reality. There are many testimonies of those who in clinical death did not want to return to the body because they perceived being in the body as a much lower and worse state.

In this way, it can be clearly seen that by leaving the body, we get closer to ourselves. In fact, we clearly see then that we did not come out of anything, that bliss rests on the insight that we were never just a physical body, but space itself and all its dimensions. All higher dimensions are within ourselves, we are made up of all the dimensions of nature. That is why we can "enter" them. And the deeper we go into them, the more we are in the "higher heaven", the closer we are to ourselves, to our true nature.

When our mind experiences leaving the body, it does not mean that we have really left the body, but that we have only become aware that our body is not the limit of our being, that what we saw from the body is the "outside world" and "higher dimensions" - actually our own being; we just weren't aware of it as ours. We had such a solid point of observation from the body that everything else seemed "outside" to us, and only that point from which we observe, the mind/ego, seemed to be inside us, as if we were only that point of observation and everything else was outside of it.

If the outer world and all dimensions of nature were not actually our being, if these two realities were separate, we would never be able to enter them. We easily enter higher dimensions every night when we dream, and every morning when we return to the physical body, simply because there is no essential difference between our inner and outer nature; the boundaries of the body are no boundaries at all. There are only limits of the mind. States of mind create the difference between waking and dreaming, between the outer and inner world.

If the outer world were not our being, not only would "out-of-body experiences" not be possible, but neither would telepathy, telekinesis, the EPR paradox, nor emotional maturity in relation to the beings of the "outer world".

"Leaving one's body" is just an illusion. We cannot leave our body because the whole of nature with all its dimensions *is* our body, our being. The experience of "leaving the body" is just dropping the illusion that we are only a body, which the mind has imposed on us.

In fact, we were never a body but a whole, the very space that enables the body and everything that exists. That is why we can never leave the body. Neither entering (incarnation) nor leaving the body (death) takes place in reality. Awakening itself is happening.

In fact, if we are going to be consistent, awakening does not happen either, because it is not a state of consciousness but consciousness itself, and the essence of consciousness is existence itself, all that is. Thus, consciousness in awakening is existence itself, the opening of the essence of existence itself, and not some new 'state of consciousness'. Awakening is returning consciousness to itself, to existence itself.

Nothing exists in space, but space itself creates everything at the moment; it takes shape as everything that exists and as all events. The manifestation of that space is consciousness. That consciousness is us. That is why we do not exist as separate individuals - real in themselves. That's why we end up loving each other when we get to know each other. We exist only as a whole, and any individuality within that whole is just a dream. And yet, because of the holographic nature of the whole, any individuality within the whole is as real as the whole itself. Each individual is a whole. Individuality should not be denied or rejected for the sake of the whole. They don't need to be distinguished. Both are one and the same.

PRACTICAL EXERCISES FOR SANCTIFYING THE EXTERIOR AS ONE'S OWN BEING

First exercise.

From the earliest times, there have been exercises for practical awareness of the exterior as one's being. These are all exercises that raise awareness of our body's energy and manage it consciously: Yoga, Tantra, Qi gong.

Energy is actually a mediator or connection between consciousness and "material" form. Consciousness shapes matter with energy; more precisely, consciousness manifests itself as matter through energy.

In addition to the physical body, we also have an energy body and a mental body. When we consciously control energy, we shape the physical body and influence physical events.

A simple example: when we exercise in the gym, we will shape the body as desired. We direct our energy and work in a certain way and it produces results. We do not spend energy on other activities that would be contrary to the given goal, but only on those that are necessary. The same applies to building a house. If we invest consciousness and energy in a certain way, we will build a house. It is the way we act on the outside world.

Energy does not exist by itself but only as a manifestation, as work, movement, act, and deed. Energy is a being in motion, in action.

In ancient times in China, the practice of working with energy was known as Qi Gong (literally translated as "working with energy"). Nowadays, Qi Gong exercises have gained popularity worldwide. In this section, we will introduce one of these exercises, which can help us consciously experience the unity of the outer and inner world. Although all Qi Gong exercises have this purpose, it seems to have been forgotten, and the exercises are often applied solely for improving health and mastering energy for better performance in the external world without revealing the true nature of the outside world. Here, we will explain a simple Qi Gong exercise in the context of the theme of this book, which is how to become aware of the outer world as our own being.

The Hun Yuan palm exercise originated from the Shaolin Monastery and was somehow transmitted to Okinawa in Japan and later to Europe. And now, it is being presented to you.

The exercise starts with relaxation, followed by standing still and fully relaxing while becoming aware of the entire surface of the body, especially the center of gravity, which is located slightly below the navel. This area is known as the *tan tien* energy center. It is logical that our energy center is also our center of gravity.

This exercise consists of three sets of movements. First, we push the space from the sides using our palms, then we raise one hand up and lower the other hand down, and finally, we raise both hands up and lower them down simultaneously. We repeat each set of movements several times according to our feeling.

***

Series 1

Stand straight, completely relaxed, as if floating. While inhaling air, raise the straightened palms of both hands to chest height, facing each other, at a distance of up to ten centimeters (1). Then, when you finish inhaling, while exhaling spread both arms at shoulder height, with the palms facing outwards, as if you are pushing two invisible walls away from you, left and right (2). When you finish exhaling, turn your palms towards each other and slowly bring them together as you inhale, feeling the resistance as if you were squeezing a big invisible ball (3). When you bring them ten centimeters closer as in the initial position, then start spreading your arms again, pushing the invisible walls while exhaling. Repeat these movements as much as you like. That's the first series in this exercise.

Series 2

When our palms are together at chest height, we continue the exercise in the other direction (4) by raising the right hand up and lowering the left hand down, palms facing opposite each other, the palm of the raised hand facing up and the lowered hand down, both in a horizontal position (5). When we finish exhaling, then inhale by lowering the right hand and raising the left. When our hands reach the height of the chest, we rotate the them at a distance of ten centimeters towards each other as if we were spinning an invisible ball (6), and then we raise the left hand and lower the right hand, with exhalation (7). We alternately raise and lower one hand and then the other, pushing the palms up and down. Again, it's as if we are separating invisible partitions, spreading them up and down with our hands. Whenever we separate our palms, we exhale; when we collect them we inhale. Repeat these movements as much as you like. That's the second series of movements in this exercise.

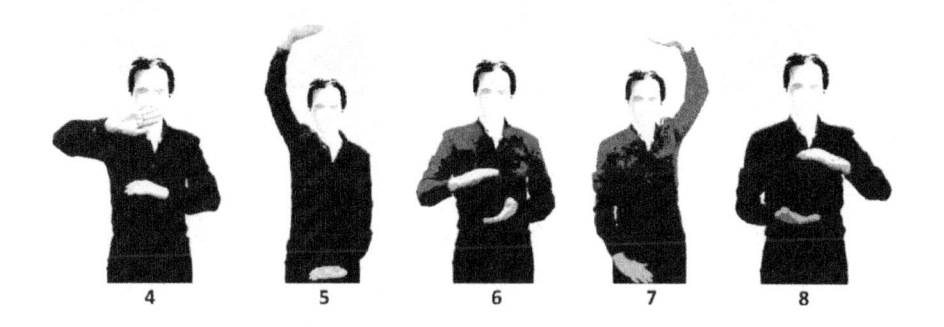

Series 3

The following variation in the exercise involves lifting and lowering both hands together with the palms facing outwards. When both hands are raised as high as possible, the palms face upwards, and when they are lowered to a horizontal position, the palms face downwards. As we lift our hands from chest height, we exhale (9), and as we lower our hands back down to chest height, we inhale (10-11). Continuing to lower our hands from chest height, we exhale (11-12). From the lowered position, we lift our hands back up to chest height, as if holding an invisible vessel, and inhale. Then, at chest height, we turn our hands upwards and exhale while raising them again (9), as if lifting an invisible vessel. We then lower them down again, as if pressing an invisible ball. Repeat these movements as many times as you like. This completes the third series of movements in this exercise.

End of exercise

When our hands are in the lower position (13), we finish the exercise by inhaling with the palms facing each other, raising them to the chest (14), then with exhalation, we finish the exercise by lowering our hands next to the body (15).

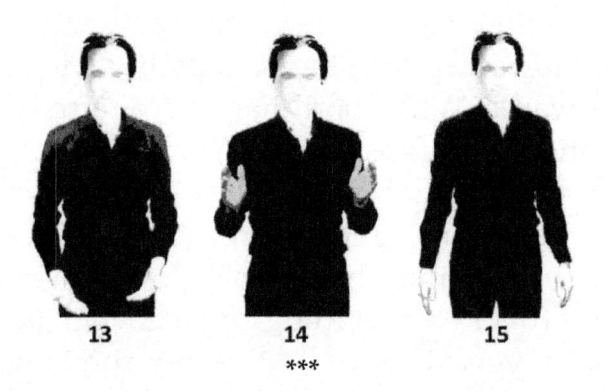

***

Practicing Qi Gong involves performing specific movements that activate our energy body and increase our awareness of invisible energy. By focusing on our breathing and relaxing our physical body, we strengthen our connection to the energy body and shift our center of gravity from the physical body to the invisible energy that surrounds us.

Unlike our daily activities that rely on muscle effort, Qi Gong emphasizes relaxation and awareness of movement and breathing. As we push the invisible walls with our palms, we also strengthen our connection to the surrounding energy, which we visualize as an invisible force that we can control and manipulate.

The key to Qi Gong is the integration of consciousness, breathing, and movement. These three elements are inherently connected, and Qi Gong helps us harmonize them and remove any mental barriers that limit our potential. By reawakening our awareness of the unity between these elements, we can tap into our full power and improve our physical, mental, and spiritual well-being.

Note the following:

- Hand movements must be coordinated with breathing. You should clearly feel how the energy from the abdomen (*tien tan*) moves towards the palms and from there goes out through the hands.

- During the entire performance, your breathing should be natural, light and deep. The rhythm of breathing must be uniform. Breathing must not be faster one time and slower the other time.

- When you raise or lower your arms, your elbows should be facing outwards.

- Knees should be straight all the time.

- Attention should always be focused on the palms.

- The exercise should be done a couple of times a day, in the morning and in the evening; you can repeat each movement group in the exercise as much as you want.

Only after the end of this exercise does the real practice begin. We do this exercise (like every *Qi Gong exercise*)only so that we can continue the practice of sanctification afterwards, throughout the day. We do neither spiritual nor physical exercises to fulfill our duty, as a ritual. Some do it that way, those are the ones who don't experience progress. All spiritual and physical exercises serve only as preparation for what we do after them, all day long. If we meditated for one hour during the day, it serves us as a preparation for meditation in all the activities of the other 23 hours.

When we do this kind of energy awareness exercise, its purpose is to make us aware of the presence of energy always and everywhere, in the space around us. After the exercise, we will feel that our palms are tingling and vibrating. When we stop the exercise and continue to do what we normally do, we do not relax our consciousness and do not indulge in spontaneous movement according to the old habit, but continue to move as if we are swimming through space; we feel everything we touch as alive, as energy that has been shaped in a material thing. Instead of the invisible wall that we pushed in the exercise and the ball that we squeezed, now we will touch things in the same way, grab clothes, perform any physical work.

We actually practice to break the habit of remaining unconscious and indulged in the activities of the body and mind as before. We sleep when we surrender to the spontaneous action of nature and external influences; they carry us like a torrent of a fallen leaf. Our mind kept us unconscious by attributing its will to that conditioned state, just as a leaf would convince itself: "I sail the stream of my own will."

We wake up when we do all the movements as a pre-conscious intention. This is so because everything exists as a conscious intention, all life and all nature. Our awakening is simply attuning to all of existence as conscious energy.

Energy is the foundation of all material things, and conscious intention is the foundation of energy. Consciousness governs energy and gives rise to physical form through intention. This is how everything we see around us, from objects to living beings and natural phenomena, came into existence. By becoming aware of the energy within us, we can also feel it outside ourselves, since everything is energy both within us and in the world around us. Everything is infused with consciousness. The consciousness that shaped nature is the same consciousness that exists within us and enables us to perceive, think, and act. Since there are no limits to energy, there are even fewer limits to consciousness, which is existence in itself.

We can only make external things aware to the extent that we are aware of them internally. This exercise teaches us to perceive everything we see and touch as a living and conscious being, whether it's our clothes, furniture, a piece of art, or a wall.

While we are familiar with the closeness we feel with loved ones, it is harder for us to extend this sense of connection to things and beings we do not love or tolerate, such as objects we consider "dead" or separate from us. Many of these things are essential to our daily lives, but we often fail to perceive them as alive and conscious.

When we wake up with the help of meditation and this exercise, then we clearly see that we breathe air only because the trees breathe it out, and that the trees breathe in what we breathe out; that the whole breathes through us. We wake up when practically and every moment we experience everything around us as ourselves. Then our every touch becomes a blessing, every word understanding, mercy and kindness the only way of life.

Energy is action. When we realize that all that exists is consciousness acting as energy, and that this consciousness exists within all of us, then we will no longer be capable of actions that are not right and good. Acting in correctness and goodness is the only way to act when we are aware of the unity of matter, energy, and consciousness. We can experience this consciousness as our essence, as the consciousness of our being. That is why we see it all around us, in everything and in every being. A soulful person is good because they see the consciousness of their being in everything outside of themselves, in everyone.

We become awakened when we realize that we exist in an ocean of conscious energy, and that we are that ocean. That consciousness becomes aware of itself through us, and we through it. It is the final phase and the realization of this exercise. At first, its action manifested itself only as heat and vibration in the palms. As we wake up, we increasingly perceive all material things around us as a part of ourselves. We become more creative and effective in everything we do, whether the question is artistic creation or simple physical work. Art is just another way to achieve the same sanctification we are talking about here. By systematically practicing sanctification, every work becomes art. Then we love every work because we see that every work is the way in which the divine consciousness is manifested. Our awareness expands to everything we come into contact with. This is experienced as a feeling of love because when energy and consciousness are recognized as one, that unity is experienced as love. Consciousness of energy outside the body, consciousness of all existence as conscious energy that has material form, can culminate in *siddhis* or "powers" with which to act outside the body - like telekinesis, for example. This will not be any "mastery of energy" or "acquisition of magical powers" but simply greater understanding and knowledge. Everyone can do what they know; what they don't know, they can't do. You know that your hand is a part of your being, that it belongs to you, and so you move it because you do not doubt it (if it were suggested under hypnosis that your hand is not yours, you would not be able to move it, even after hypnosis). You will also be able to move objects around the table without touching them, just by understanding that they are also an integral part of your being. Right now, you are just hypnotized by not knowing who you really are, that the outside world is outside of you, and that you are alienated and powerless.

Before, we were emotionally attached to some things, mostly to memories, but also to beautiful and useful things. Now we will feel love for the whole of existence.

Before, we were attracted by love only to certain persons. Now we will feel it towards all living beings. Certainly, we will not need to hug and kiss strangers around us, as Meher Baba did, but we will express our love in all the other constructive ways in which it should be expressed. Through useful work and help in various forms; through understanding above all. Love gives the deepest possible understanding because it is the awareness of the energy that connects everything. Love is above the mind. The mind can only understand what is logically and empirically experienced. Love connects into a higher sense everything that seems disconnected and illogical, love forgives everything that the mind condemns. Love is the consciousness of the soul, therefore it is above the mind and the entire physical world. Love always gives and asks for nothing. Love is the true hidden goal and motive of everything we do in this world. It is the basis of the life energy that we are conscious of. Do you think that something else drives your heart and your breathing other than the unconditional love of the space (ether) that creates your every moment?

The basis of life is the division of DNA. DNA division is done with the help of proteins. The code for the creation of proteins is in the DNA itself. It is scientific proof that higher consciousness makes life possible, not material causality, and that life manifests as unconditional love.

***

Second exercise.
Staring at the sun.

The sun has always awakened all living beings. In order to wake up, we only need to become aware of the whole process and to fully participate in it. In order to truly participate in it, we must first understand it. In previous chapters, we have already stated that photons create matter. This practically means that light creates matter and all life. It also means that light is not just a simple illumination and removal of darkness, but a carrier of information. Photons from the stars carry information for the formation of matter and all life. The practice of gazing into the sun represents a radical transition from intellectual reflection on what photons do to direct insight into their action within ourselves and in the world around us. With this exercise, we directly experience that light becomes our body and mind, that it is every movement we make, that it manifests as the earth and all life, everything that exists. This direct experience is realized very simply: by looking directly at the sun, by allowing the sun itself to open the insight of cognition in us, to wake us up.

It can also be practiced by looking directly at the rising or setting sun, in the period up to one hour after sunrise and before sunset. Then the sunlight is weaker and you can watch without danger to your eyesight. Each day, the viewing time increases by ten seconds until we reach 45 minutes of continuous viewing.

On the first day, during safe hours, watch for a maximum of 10 seconds. After that, cover your eyes with your palms for a few minutes to rest from the light. On the second day, watch the sunrise or sunset for 20 seconds and add 10 seconds each day. Thus, at the end of 10 consecutive days of looking at the sun, you will look at the sun for 100 seconds, i.e., 1 minute and 40 seconds.

It is very important to have a notebook and keep detailed time records. (There is also an application for mobile phones called "Sungazing Timer")

In this way, by gradually adding 10 seconds with each new practice, one can reach 45 minutes of sungazing per session. It will take approximately 270 days to achieve this goal, but given that it may not be possible to practice every day due to inclement weather or other reasons, it may take 2 to 3 years to complete the entire exercise.

Once you have reached 45 minutes of sungazing per session on the 270th day, it is recommended to gradually reduce the duration of each session by one minute per day until you reach 15 minutes. This will allow you to gradually transition out of the practice while still maintaining the benefits. Those 15 minutes can be used as an occasional exercise in the future, when you need to recharge with solar energy.

To practice sungazing, stand with your back straight on bare ground, stones, or warm concrete with bare feet, as grounding is important for connecting the body's electricity with the ground. Avoid standing on grass, which absorbs energy.

You can blink your eyes during the practice and move your gaze around the sun in circles or by looking left and right, up and down, as long as the sunlight enters your eyes. Only look directly at the sun when it is weak enough and it feels safe to do so.

It is not necessary to stare directly at the bright sun. What's important is that sunlight enters the eyes at any angle and contacts the hemoglobin in the blood of the retina. Hemoglobin in human blood has a similar composition to chlorophyll in plants, and it plays a role in turning sunlight into energy. The retina of the eye is the only place in the human body where blood comes into direct contact with light. It has been estimated that in 45 minutes, all the blood in the body passes through the eye, and that through sungazing, all the blood is exposed to the sun.

Detailed instructions on sungazing can be found in the chapter on Prayer of my book *Religiousness: Instructions for Use*. These instructions are based on the practices of solar yogis Hira Ratan Manek and Sunyogi Umasankar, and include additional details not found in their teachings.

Sunlight is the source of all life, and without cosmic radiation, an embryo cannot develop. Therefore, it is more accurate to say that outer space, through the light of the stars, creates all forms of life and existence. Even the stars themselves derive their energy from space.

Therefore, we look at the sun in order to receive the light and with it the energy of the sun in the deepest way. That is the first factor.

The second factor is our awareness. We are always exposed to the sun during the day, but we don't pay attention to it unless it is too strong, or we haven't had good weather for a long time. By looking at the sun, we fully engage our awareness. This means that through our body we completely actualize the process that occurs in nature.

The sun illuminates the earth and life is born. However, when we stand with our bare feet and look at the sun, the sunlight does not connect directly with the earth, but through our being, through our awareness. Then the sunlight consciously merges with the earth. Unlike the rest of nature, that event becomes conscious in us. We consciously participate in the creation of life and that is what awakens us in this exercise. This is how a new quality is created that did not exist in nature until then. When something is realized, then it is realized. The meaning of the existence of the sun, and the stars in general, is realized when their action becomes fully conscious by the witness who is our soul. Then the divine consciousness manifests and realizes itself completely. We help that realization by our testimony or conscious participation. The witness plays the role of the bottom in the container with which the water is collected. It's a round thing with a bottom that prevents water from falling through. If there was no bottom, the water could not be contained. Consciousness as a witness is like a bottom that holds water. ***Self-awareness is a factor that prevents the events of nature from proceeding blindly and unconsciously.***

On the other hand, such realization of the natural process is what awakens us. When we consciously engage in the cosmic process of the arrival of sunlight on earth; when we carry it through ourselves, feel it and fully experience it, then we become an integral part of that process. When we experience ourselves as part of the whole, it awakens us.

We have already said that we are awakened only by an insight into the true nature of reality. The true nature of reality is awareness itself. There is really no more direct way to engage in the process of realizing reality than by looking at the sun with the understanding outlined here. You only need to feel it deeply enough and it will carry you like a wave into permanent alertness. You will see the sun as the source of your being, your consciousness; it will always be available to you; you will not be able to forget it. The classic problem for all meditators is that they forget the state of pure consciousness they achieve in meditation and therefore have to repeat it. When you recognize pure consciousness in being and all existence, and when you see its source, the sun, light, space, then you will never be able to lose the pure consciousness of your soul, it will be present everywhere, like the light of the sun, like space, like everything that happens inside and outside of you. All of this will be one event, so that any difference between the outer and inner world will disappear.

Sungazing reaches its peak when all distinction between sunlight and any physical form disappears for the practitioner, when their body and every movement and all of nature becomes condensed light (which it is). That's how the sun wakes up a person. It has been scientifically proven that matter is created from photons, light. When someone directly experiences that fundamental law of nature, they will be awakened. When an awakened individual sees the essence of a physical form, then they see its aura, and they see the form as light.

In addition to all this, looking at the sun is extremely beneficial for health. First of all, psychological depression disappears very quickly, and with prolonged practice, physical health improves as well. It is a method that can cure even the most serious, supposedly "incurable" disease.

What individuals will immediately notice is that by looking at the sun, intuition is greatly increased. If one has any doubts and questions, the answers can come during or right after the practice.

Third exercise.

You can combine these two exercises into one. While looking at the sun you can practice *Qi Gong*. The effect will be greatly increased.

Proposal for a fourth exercise.

Staring at the sun and experiencing the union of heaven and earth through you can be greatly enhanced by the practice *of tantra.* Just as through the exercise of looking at the sun you can experience how the sky and the earth merge through you as light, so the practice of *tantra* makes you aware of the merging of beings of the opposite sex (only the exchange of energy of the opposite sexes brings the experience of psychoenergetic wholeness; it is a law of nature and not someone's conviction). You can combine these two experiences into one that will be very effective. It is necessary that while looking at the sun, while you are aware of the unity of earth and sky in your being, you should experience the same unity with another person, a partner in *tantra,* or a loved one. Just having physical contact while looking at the sun together is enough.

With every physical contact, energy is exchanged between two beings. That's why physical touch is so important and needed by everyone. Certainly, the greater the contact, the greater the energy and consciousness along with it. That is why a completely physical contact, i.e. sexual intercourse, was ideal for the practice of gazing at the sun together. With the mandatory grounding of both participants, this is not a *tantra exercise* in the sun, but a combination of solar yoga and *tantra*. Therefore, we need a complete experience of the unity of the energy of the sun and the earth in our being through grounding, and the unity of the energy of the opposite poles through bodily union.

If we consider a man and woman as heaven and earth in miniature (which is close to Taoist philosophy), then the experience of looking at the sun is multiplied by tantric practice, just as tantric practice is multiplied by looking at the sun. Both practices have the same underlying psychoenergetic process.

UNDERSTANDING THE MEANING OF MERGING THE OUTER AND INNER WORLD

The outer and inner worlds have never been separate, but are only fictitiously separated by our minds and egos for the purpose of action in the physical body. We can only act in the physical world when we have individuality and know what we are doing as individuals. The mind and ego therefore have a protective function that allows us to exist and act as conscious individuals.

The birth of the soul in the individual body occurs so that the absolute divine consciousness, which is all that exists, is recognized in every relative form in all that can be.

The essence of that process is hidden in the details. It is a process in which divine consciousness, through the human soul in the body, becomes aware of all its possibilities and actions. The individual human soul perceives these possibilities as its own karma, meaning actions and the consequences of actions on consciousness, awareness of the action itself and the consequences of each action. This awareness exists only within the framework of a mind and ego; that is, in individual action.

This awareness takes place in all aspects - from understanding atoms and subatomic particles to the reasons for World War I and II (did those wars follow the discovery of atomic energy?) to the psychological reasons you keep forgetting your house keys (because you don't feel good in your home) and all the richness of karmic dramas and soul consciousness presented in the works of Dostoevsky, Goethe, Shakespeare, Schelling, Novalis, and J.S. Bach.

In the consciousness of the soul, the meaning of all possible events is unified. This unification reaches its climax and finale in the realization of the unity of the outer and inner worlds.

However, since the unity of outer and inner already exists, and only our mind separates them for practical reasons of acting in this world, there are times when the mind and ego give way in their protective function, when they disintegrate temporarily or permanently. Then a person can experience the unity of the outer and the inner in a spontaneous and uncontrolled way. This fills them with the bliss of the highest knowledge, they experience an "oceanic feeling". It seems very attractive; in fact it is the greatest attractive force a person can feel. When they experience it spontaneously, they can remain permanently enchanted by it. This is the case with the so-called "holy lunatics intoxicated by God," who were respected in all ancient cultures, especially the East. In the rational West, such people generally ended up in insane asylums. They have an experience of unity, they see the higher dimensions of nature, but they do not know how to express their awareness of this in a correct, constructive, and effective way. They do not understand the meaning of all this happening.

Understanding the meaning is the real goal of life; that is, the incarnation of the soul's consciousness into a physical body. Understanding the meaning is actually connecting the absolute divine consciousness with every possible manifestation of it, from the largest to the smallest, from what seems the most important to everything that seems the most unimportant. When such an all-encompassing consciousness occurs in an awakened individual, when everything is connected to the whole, then the absolute divine consciousness is fully actualized in all its possibilities.

Everything that happens in the universe (which happens as the universe itself) is the actualization of divine consciousness. This happens only in a person's realization of their essence, the soul, which is a holographic reflection of the divine whole. Everything else, the entire outer universe, serves only as a means for this to happen. A person combines the absolute and the relative into meaning, into unity. They do this through all their work, through civilization and culture. They succeed in this in a rational and logical way as much as they are aware of their soul. A person's task is only to manifest the original unity of divine consciousness in a rational and logical way through science, with scientific precision and effectiveness. Science will be the religion of the future to the extent that it accepts and manifests the consciousness of the divine soul.

That's why the consciousness of unity does not mean that you will just sail on a cloud of bliss across a flower meadow, that you will see yourself in everything around you and welcome a car rushing towards you on the road with open arms, that you will explain to some Taliban (a young, immature soul) what he is doing wrong. No. **Awakening only means more understanding of natural laws and karma. Nothing else.** If you are alert, you will avoid the car; even better, you won't get in its way, where you shouldn't be. You will do what you need to do to avoid collisions. You will learn to build a car and to drive it. As an awakened one, you will do everything in accordance with natural laws, and better than ever. You will leave all the Taliban of this world at a safe distance to experience the consequences of their actions, and you will help them only as much as it is necessary for them to collide with them faster.

SOME MORE TECHNICAL DETAILS ABOUT AWAKENING

We are all aware that our state of consciousness is constantly in flux, with our moods and emotions changing every day in cycles and rhythms. Meditation practitioners throughout history have observed that the peace and alertness they attain through meditation is easily disturbed by the challenges and events of daily life. Therefore, meditation must be a consistent practice in order to establish its benefits.

Even if we achieve a brief moment of alertness, it quickly dissipates as we become swept up in the course of daily events and seemingly fall into a lucid dream state. We participate in these events, but in the background, we know we were awake and independent of them. However, we soon forget this awareness and fall back into the sleep of everyday life, only realizing we were in a dream when we wake up next time. Even if we make a promise to maintain awakening and self-awareness continuously, we quickly forget after only a few minutes.

The temptation of the opposite, while not negative, is crucial in expanding our perception and breaking the limitations we impose on ourselves in our comfort zones. It presents us with experiences and challenges that we would not seek out on our own, confronting us with unknown realities that shatter the illusions of our mind. We need this expansion of perception more than we realize.

The expansion of perception that arises from experiencing opposites is the key to awakening, rather than insisting on a singular type of experience or awareness. Only when we maintain self-awareness and awakening continuously, 24 hours a day, seven days a week, and throughout a lunar cycle of 28 days, can we become permanently awake. This is achievable only when we sufficiently expand our perception through experiencing all opposites.

The effort exists only until we distinguish our awakening (our awareness of ourselves) from existence and from ourselves - until we understand the unique basis of existence that is behind all opposites. When we understand what awareness really is - that it is existence itself(our essence)that everything is consciousness and that everything is *our* consciousness, then all effort to wake up disappears. Then we surrender to her like a wave that carries us. Therefore, effort disappears and we become truly awake when we perfectly understand the true nature of existence - when we stop resisting it. Simple, right? It is similar to a game of tug-of-war: the more we strain to be aware, the more difficult it becomes for us, because we are also on the other side of the rope, awareness is already all there is. Consciousness is as effortless as the infinite space that makes everything possible. Any effort to be conscious is a symptom that we are unconscious, that we are in conflict with consciousness, that we do not understand the true nature of consciousness.

We will not succeed in awakening as long as we try to do it in a certain way, with some certain "spiritual practice". We will succeed when we accept that our entire existence awakens us in all possible ways, that life itself is a process of awakening, when we stop interfering with things as they are, and when we accept them as perfect at every moment. Correct meditation, as pure transcendence, is helping to accept reality in such a way.

Every method and every effort implies achieving some kind of change or goal. Awakening is knowing the reality that is every moment.

We are not awake and we have to strain and fight with everything and everyone just because we believe too much in the fictions of our mind, its virtual reality. The mind with its thoughts is a wall that separates us from seeing true reality. Whenever we have thoughts in our head, we look at that wall, at the shadows that appear on it, and we play in shows we consider to be life and reality. We look at our own plays. We can see the true reality only when we are without thoughts, with a clear, open mind. Those are the moments when our breath stops as we look in wonder, when our mind "stops". Although these are only moments for us, they remain forever in us as a source of bliss.

We can give an apt comparison here.

Pure space or ether, the quantum field, every moment creates its opposite, a primary particle that instantly transforms into all possible particles and atoms, which further transform into larger structures, molecules, elements that make up the physical world and life as we know it. In the quantum field, pure space, there is no time and space as we know it here. The laws of nature of the physical world arise only when elementary particles combine into larger structures. Our reality is the reality of the great elements. That is why linear time and causality rule in our reality, but not in pure space.

Our being is a microcosm, a small reflection of the cosmos, and everything that happens in the universe happens in parallel within us. The pure space of the ether is equivalent to our self-awareness, the consciousness of our soul, and when it vibrates, thoughts arise, which become our virtual reality. This virtual reality of our mind is necessary to comprehend the physical world more easily, but it also suppresses our pure self-awareness, relegating it to the background. Understanding this technical description can help us awaken. Since everything arises from our pure consciousness, all the elements of nature and life, as well as our thoughts, are manifestations of the same space.

Therefore, everything we perceive and think should be the subject of meditation, focused attention, with the goal of sanctification or awakening. There is no need for special facilities or times for meditation, as everything in life is an opportunity to awaken. Life itself is a process of awakening, and the whole world is one big wakefulness. However, we remain asleep because we imagine that the world is something else and that we are something other than that world.

To achieve true awakening, we must be fully present in reality as it is in each moment, without projecting our own version of reality onto it. This requires the disappearance of our minds, which are the source of disturbance and confusion in reality. From the moment we become conscious individuals, we create disturbances by imagining that reality is separate from us and not our essence. This separation from reality is only overcome when we recognize that every thought in our head originates from the divine absolute, and that we never existed as separate beings. True awareness arises when the idea of our individual existence disappears, and we realize that only the divine whole exists. This description of reality may not be popular, but it can inspire us on our path towards awakening. It is important to know where we are going.

We should also know that there are places and circumstances that help us to be more awake, as well as places and circumstances that narrow our consciousness and throw us into lower states, which make us negative.

Both are equally attractive. We will begin to truly awaken when we permanently choose what is best for us.

Knowledge of the science of astrology can greatly help in understanding the circumstances and challenges that narrow our consciousness and the circumstances that elevate our consciousness. Astrology actually serves as an aid in understanding one's own path to awakening; it is an individual manual for awakening. Here we will only mention one specific detail: you should know that the point 150 degrees in front of our Sun is the place that provides us with the best conditions for awakening. You need to know in which house that point is located, that house (field) will be the area of life that suits us best for awakening. If it is the sixth house, then work will be the area that brings us the most awareness, that brings us the best experiences necessary for awakening, not only work as such, but also the workplace itself. If it is the tenth house, then it will be a career, working on a career will be connected with our awakening, the highest awareness. If it is the seventh, then marriage and partnership, public exposure. If the eleventh, then one of our friends, our social life will be the key factor in our awakening. And so on. It is necessary to connect the nature of the house in which the sun is located with the nature of the house in which there is a point 150 degrees away from the sun. We need to dedicate ourselves more to those areas of life if we want to wake up easier.

SUDDEN AND GRADUAL AWAKENING

Throughout history, two methods of awakening have existed. The gradual method involves working on oneself through meditative discipline and study. In contrast, the sudden method shatters the mind immediately and enables the breakthrough of soul consciousness and awareness of reality's true nature. The mind has always obscured reality by pretending to be the only means of revealing it. Transcendence of the mind reveals reality, which can happen suddenly through certain techniques or gradually through the understanding of meaning and transcendence itself.

Sudden awakening is appealing to people because it removes the illusion that we need to achieve, change, build, or discover something. It reveals that we are always what we should be, and the highest reality is always present, although we might not have seen it because we were caught up in our imaginations. In Zen, *koans* bring the mind into a paradoxical situation, stopping it and allowing insight to open, transcending the mind and enabling the higher consciousness to manifest itself. Other methods, such as those used in Sufism, involve bringing the body and mind into a trance, creating a crack in the mind's flow for insight into unity consciousness to break through. Psychedelic substances such as ayahuasca and DMT can also be used to transcend the mind, allowing the consciousness of the soul to manifest and provide insights. Depending on karmic maturity, these insights can be colored by various contents, but they can also bring a direct insight into the highest reality.

However, the problem with sudden awakening is that its effects soon wear off. Although a strong impression of knowledge remains, it cannot be maintained without discipline and understanding of reality's meaning. Merely seeing and experiencing reality is not enough; we must understand its meaning in all possible aspects, which has always been called "wisdom insight." Awakening involves a complete understanding of all the reasons why we are not awake and why we need to wake up. It is the basic theme of everyone's life in this world. If one loses the boundaries of mind and ego without understanding why they have them, they might end up in an unpleasant place with metal bars on the windows. These will be new boundaries imposed for security reasons.

That's why gradual awakening has an advantage. It develops discipline and provides more small insights that gradually reveal the bigger picture of reality. The gradual method is gradual because for each insight it first makes sense before moving on. You can't take the next step on that path if you haven't determined well with complete understanding the day before. Only understanding takes you further.

In correct meditation we reach a pure awareness of reality, then in activity we continue to recognize it in everything we do, but at a much lower intensity and we often lose it. However, we gradually connect consciousness with action, and this gradually brings us understanding, and the deepest awareness of ourselves and activities in the outer world. Awakening occurs when we finally stop distinguishing the pure awareness of ourselves from the outer world, from existence itself. Then we don't give up anything, neither the world nor ourselves. It is one and the same thing: neither is the world something outside, nor is our individuality real in itself. There is no world or ego, there is nothing to give up; nothing to become. Samsara is nirvana – nirvana is samsara; form is emptiness, emptiness is form. The only illusion that has ever existed is the distinction and separation of form and emptiness, consciousness and existence, emphasizing one at the expense of the other.

That's the problem with sudden awakening. Without the discipline and moderation that brings the deepest insight, sudden awakening has the great attraction of a quick solution to a problem, but also the illusion that we have freed ourselves from some illusion, some burden. Freedom from illusion is also illusion because illusion is that which does not exist. Those who thus experience an awakening as an awakening from the illusion of the world, have a tendency to declare the world and life an illusion, something bad from which they have freed themselves. They see it as a big change.

However, this is only the impression that the consciousness of the soul has left on the mind. Like when we suddenly come out of the dark into bright light and it blinds us. Those who experience a sudden awakening can also be blinded. They no longer see the world simply because of the contrast with which the consciousness of the soul acts on the mind. Only with gradual getting used to the consciousness of the soul, understanding what it is and what the world is (that they are one and the same), can it be clearly seen that the world was never a problem, because it was never different from us - from the consciousness with which we knew the world. Only to the extent that we are alienated from ourselves and our essence are we also alienated from the world. Our inner alienation and unconsciousness is reflected on the outside.

The gradual awakening is quiet and simple, like the growth of a tree. It doesn't go anywhere, everything is in it, it doesn't ask for anything, it just opens up until it blossoms. This is what happens to a person who gradually awakens with a full understanding of wakefulness. Each degree of his gradualness has the value of a sudden awakening, but he does not make a drama about it, he clearly sees that "with the highest awakening he has not achieved anything new" (Buddha's words). He clearly sees that the highest reality has always been his essence. What else could it be?

Perfect awakening is perfectly imperceptible.

INDIVIDUAL AND COLLECTIVE AWAKENING

There has long been confusion about whether human awakening is an individual or collective phenomenon, whether these are so related that individual awakening can trigger a collective awakening, or if collective awakening affects the individual. Both processes exist, but it is necessary to understand them correctly. They are separate and distinct, even though they lead to the same goal.

Individual awakening is essentially the complete actualization of soul consciousness without obstacles or distortions. The average human life happens in a state of distorted or reduced soul consciousness. That is why the average human life consists of illusions and ignorance, conflicts and mistakes, and overall suffering. All life incarnations serve to train soul consciousness to express itself correctly within the conditions of the physical world and all possibilities of existence. One life is not enough because of all the possibilities. That is why we talk about a multitude of lives, reincarnation, and the karmic maturation of soul consciousness. The fully mature soul in a human body becomes aware of itself in an absolute sense; that is, it awakens, knows who it is and what it is like independently of the birth and death of the incarnated body. Then rebirth becomes unnecessary. The soul recognizes itself as the pure space of the absolute, which is all that is, was, and will ever be; that this space is the essence and the potential for all things; that nothing exists apart from it, which is why the soul does not exist as something special and separate, and it sees that it is the very source of all possible existence.

In other words, individual awakening comes with the realization of who we were before our birth, independent of body and mind. We become objectively aware of our own essence and existence as it actually is. When we identify with the body, we remain subjectively aware, limited, and in ignorance.

To a greater or lesser extent, objective consciousness of the soul manifests constantly in many people. It just doesn't happen at full potential as did Buddha's awakening. This is the source for all those strong feelings and insights that move people to their greatest and best deeds, and for all those great expressions of divine love expressed through people. Especially parental love, which every being needs most and all people seek throughout their lives in all their relationships. In human experience, parental love is the only direct expression of divine love, which is actually the energy of life. In addition to love, soul consciousness is expressed through all possible forms of creativity, which means the unlimited creation of new experience as the content of life.

To a greater or lesser extent, most people experience these individual manifestations of soul consciousness. They can be spontaneous but are integral to every culture. The highest culture of individual self-knowledge that is not spontaneous occurs in the discipline described in Patanjali's *Yoga Sutras*, in the teachings of early Buddhism, and in esoteric Christianity. These present a method of systematic cultivation that can turn individual experience into a collective one.

***

Collective awakening is different, although it can be somewhat compared to individual maturation. It can be said that collective awakening is the achievement of objective soul consciousness through humane social organization, correct interpersonal relations, and the understanding of natural laws (science).

Manifesting consciousness of the soul through interpersonal relationships means a complete recognition of consciousness as the basis of life, which is the same in all living beings, in all people, in all existence. This is a complete fulfillment of the basic ethical principle that says, "do not do to others what you do not want done to you". Such action realizes the principle of non-violence. Also, acting from soul consciousness always generates a completely correct action without any coercion by law or obligation. From soul consciousness, we act rightly only because the act is right. Acting from soul consciousness is always correct and humane because the divine consciousness of the soul is in everything that exists. *The correctness of individual action reflects the recognition and alignment of the individual's soul consciousness with the absolute divine consciousness.* That is why it is impossible for such an individual to act destructively or wrongly. Soul consciousness sees itself in everything and thereby sees what is right and wrong. We can say it is clairvoyant in its correctness. To a lesser extent, this is known as intuition, conscience, the "path of the heart", or the "insight of wisdom" (*jnana*).

Although such soul consciousness is reached through individual maturation, a sufficient social arrangement becomes necessary for enabling such consciousness to be accepted as the norm in everyday life. Without sufficient soul consciousness enabling correct action, the law of the stronger rules, and in order to sufficiently regulate life in such conditions, laws and punishments must be enacted. Lao Tzu said: "When the great Tao was lost, laws and customs appeared." (Tao Te Jing, 18) *The great Tao* is the consciousness of our soul.

External cultivation is perceived by the naive human mind as a conspiracy against his soul and freedom - as coercion. External cultivation is like that, but it has a justifiable reason for existence. A child may endure orders from his parents that are meant only for his own good, but the child may only perceive them as coercive and restrictive. This is similar to raising the human race on planet Earth, a much more difficult experience.

The problem is that soul consciousness is the greatest attractive force for people. It connects us both with nature and with the divine; it connects our human essence with absolute freedom. Everyone experiences absolute freedom as their essence and source of purpose, primarily through unconditional love. If not the reality for most people in this world, it is still the ideal they aspire to, whether they are aware of it or not. Those who behave violently and destructively do so because they suffer from the lack of ideal love.

Immature and unconscious people may also strive for absolute freedom, but problems come because their striving manifests itself unconsciously and often turns destructive. Young, immature souls do not distinguish destructiveness, spontaneity, and unconsciousness from true freedom, which is the essential quality of the absolute and the highest fruit of consciousness. They often think that expressing freedom means to be wild and wanton and doing stupid things.

Immature people are attracted to the absolute through nature, and therefore they think their purpose is always to remain the same in nature - without further development. That is why immature people need coercion that will force them to learn and develop, to recognize with scientific precision - concretely and effectively - the consciousness of the absolute in everything.

***

Thus, in humans, individual self-realization of divine consciousness occurs as God-realization or enlightenment. In the world, in humankind, this same self-realization of divine consciousness occurs collectively through the spiritual and material culture, through the improvement of civilization through science and technology, art, human rights, and freedom.

Collective awakening takes place through the knowledge of natural laws, science, and the application of such knowledge throughout the world in a free and correct manner.

In this world, scientific knowledge serves to express consciousness of the soul correctly and precisely on the physical plane so that it can operate in nature. It clearly cannot do so when people do not know the natural laws.

Before science, the creative activity of soul consciousness was expressed through art. The development of art has always accompanied the development of material culture, sometimes preceding it. Art has always reflected the intelligence and imagination that first shaped the physical world, that designed and connected experiences no mind could design or connect. Art unites the transcendental world of ideas with the physical world and helps to shape the physical world through ideas. This is most visible in the development of design throughout history. The more intelligent and perfect the development of design, the more correctly the divine consciousness of the human soul manifests in our physical world, which itself was entirely created by the intelligent design of the divine consciousness.

However, this process for the correct manifestation of soul consciousness in our world has not yet crossed half its path toward realization. Hence, much unrest and chaos covers the world. It is important to know at what stage of development we exist in this moment so we do not naively idealize our condition and expect the impossible (as is the case with those who demand free energy in order to enjoy even more the lowest passions and destructive illusions.)

On this planet, we struggle over how soul consciousness will manifest itself.

The human soul has a problem with manifesting at such a low level - where we are currently - because it originates from the divine absolute - all that is. Soul consciousness itself is always complete and perfect; it does not need anything. However, there is inertia of soul consciousness in man until one becomes fully conscious. In this world, such inertia is manifested individually - after enlightenment or God-realization - in those who no longer want anything from this world, who become independent from everything in the world, who sometimes choose to live in caves. Many saints have lived like this. The best example from recent times is Bhagavan Sri Ramana Maharshi.

On a collective level, the attractive power of soul consciousness has expressed itself in cultures and civilizations that achieved sufficient development to live peacefully and beautifully and simply enjoy existence itself in unity with nature. These civilizations were religious in the right way and did not distinguish their spirituality from nature itself; that is, from existence. Such were the old pre-Christian religions that lasted thousands of years without any major change.

The problem is, if people with human souls had been left to live as they wished, they would still be living in log cabins and using horses for transportation. That would be enough for them. Material culture and civilization would not have developed. In order for such to develop, there needed to be a negative force that made creative soul consciousness work as if it were its first time here, to develop from the beginning - step by step - as if it needed to create something new. Throughout history, this force ultimately suppressed old tribal structures that had firmly guarded their traditions, which had not changed for centuries. Replacing village shamans and druids, who solved all social and personal problems, universities were opened and literacy was universally spread (Royal Society of London for Improving Natural Knowledge, 1662). Initially, that force was provided by Judeo-Christianity, which in every way suppressed centuries old pre-Christian faiths (often under the rubric of "a witch hunt") and thereby initiated and imposed our modern world of material culture and science.[12]

This compulsion for the development of material culture creates a paradoxical and incomprehensible situation for the soul, because the soul originates from the Absolute, where everything already exists as timeless. Many people still come into conflict with this new age in their attempts to preserve tradition. Tradition represents a mode of behavior proven to be successful for a given society over time, and any successful behavior is difficult to

---

[12] Magic has the power to act, but only on an individual level. Only talented individuals with esoteric knowledge can be successful magicians (shamans and druids). Science represents the power of action on a collective level; it is universally applicable. That is why the future development of humanity lies in the development of science, not magic. This was correctly understood in 1662 by the founders of the Royal Society, who were the greatest magicians and alchemists of their time - led by Isaac Newton. Instead of belief in spirits (which exist), Philosophiæ Naturalis Principia Mathematica was introduced in 1687.

change. Tradition may be good for young souls needing guidance in their actions, but it becomes problematic for a modern world changing faster than our ability to change traditional behavior. Tradition then becomes a conservatism that rejects all change due to fear and misunderstanding of the new. The essence of manifesting soul consciousness lies in freedom and creativity, which means discovering and creating new things through challenges and risk. Conservative traditions do not allow for that.

The individual soul falls into oblivion of its identity when it is born into a body, where it must learn to manifest soul consciousness during its growth and maturation in the new body. Something similar happens on the collective level for the entire human race.

The problem comes in maintaining a balance between soul consciousness, which must be preserved in order for people to know who they are, and learning about the world in all its scientific detail so that soul consciousness manifests appropriately.

Soul consciousness in this world must be preserved, but to the extent and manner it does not hinder material development with its own self-satisfied inertia; that is, only enough to encourage development.

In fact, all effort boils down to making a person aware of their true purpose in this world. Due to the great strength of a soul, when one finds themselves in this conditioned world, they spontaneously aspire to return to their true source, to the "heavenly kingdom" (the essential aspiration of Gnostics and Orthodox Christians), to liberation from the sufferings of this world (the aspiration of Buddhists), or to spontaneously giving priority to God in everything (the aspiration of Muslims). This spontaneous aspiration of the soul to return to its original divine state is expressed in the conservative religions of Judaism, Orthodox Christianity, Buddhism, and Islam. Some individuals reject technological development altogether and find their ideal life in nature or villages far away from cities. Such aspirations are wrong because they do not accord with the overall plan for this world that all souls brought with them. Since they are already here, souls must realize why they are here and should not immediately turn back because conditions are difficult (they are difficult only because of the misbehaviors as described; because these souls remain in conflict with nature and its purpose). Going back to avoid the world is the wrong aspiration because so much effort and so many resources have been invested in this entire game and its setting. Not just on planet Earth, but throughout the entire solar system, all of which was made to serve the grand plan (according to Gnostic teachings). Not only that, but all this was done specifically and deliberately by our souls before 'descending' into this physical world. They created all the conditions for their incarnations, and these conditions do not apply only to the physical body, but to the entire lifetime conditions and actions of a given physical body.

Therefore, avoiding material culture and technological development is avoidance of the very goal for which our souls came into this world, the purpose for which they created this world. Material culture is but a continuation of their original creation. Spirituality is not found in avoidance of the material world but in discovery of the spiritual within it, of the divine within the material. The soul becomes conscious by discovering there is no matter separate to itself, but that the entire objective world is the divine consciousness itself.

We return to our true nature by moving forward, getting to know and perfect the world with our own perfection and creativity, not by running away from all the difficulties and challenges that are necessary prerequisites for creativity.

This is why there is eternal war in the world regarding the balance between our soul's awareness of itself and our work developing material culture and civilization - the balance between our immature desire to return to original security and our need to move forward through risk in order to discover the new and unknown.

This conflict regarding the imbalance between the attractive power of soul consciousness and our work in the world is reflected in the conflict between Eastern and Western civilization; in conflict between tradition and progress; in the clash between forces leading the "New World Order" and traditional people who love their family and republic, sovereignty; in NATO's conflict with Russia; in the conflict between false and true history; in the conflict between Catholicism and Orthodox Christianity, and in the conflict of the modern world with the Muslim world.

Essentially, all wars are fought over this higher work ethic. Young, immature souls do not possess it, which is why conservatism and tradition suits them; they feel safe and protected in such, where everything is provided for them in life. Like children, they expect God to provide them with everything. Meanwhile, a small group of mature souls acts to create new values and to perfect material culture while also trying to perfect and develop this higher work ethic in those who do not possess it. Young souls avoid creating material culture. They simply use what they find, like little children. One group pulls back and the other pulls forward. Neither group understands the whole process described here. Misunderstanding the higher process at work, they kill each other, labeling each other as "primitive" or as "infidels alienated from God". Both groups forget that culture spreads through culture and not through lies, wars and genocide.[13] One should not be killed for their immaturity, just as parents do not kill their young because they are immature and difficult to raise.[14] In reality, we all need each other. Material development without soul consciousness becomes a cruel gladiatorial arena (typified by the English), while soul consciousness without material development remains immature, primitive, and unconscious (typified by the Russians).

Material development accomplished through creative and scientific work, using higher work ethics based on human rights and freedom, is the only proper way to raise soul consciousness within the material plane.

The Fourth Industrial Revolution is about to start, but the highest ideals of most people are still mental concepts created in the Middle Ages and before.

At first glance, it might seem as if such great differences between the most primitive societies (cultures) and the most developed - which live in close proximity with mixing due to immigration - would present insurmountable problems for further development. Some heartless individuals see the solution to this problem in the "golden billion".

---

[13] Stuart Laycock: All the Countries We've Ever Invaded: And the Few We Never Got Round To (2012)

[14] Certainly there exist immature people and peoples who cannot change. Their role is to remain as they are in order to create experiences not possible otherwise. For these, we have legitimate measures to limit them, and legal penalties for their infractions. We are addressing here the principles of development that should be adhered to if we want to become fully civilized and humane.

The problem with such a wrong view that causes conflict between nations and cultures is in misunderstanding the true nature of soul consciousness. Soul consciousness is never one-sided; it cannot be reached by suppressing unconsciousness - considered its opposite – or as spirituality versus materialism. Soul consciousness transcends all opposites, which is precisely why opposites are necessary to its experience. Soul consciousness manifests more clearly when its capacity for experience is greater; it becomes greater when the opposites experienced are greater; that is, with greater diversity among people and their experiences. This experience with opposites expands and increases our capacity for perception, and only this greater capacity for perception of all experience increases our level of soul consciousness.

Soul consciousness sees variety and difference as the wealth of divine possibility, not as a problem to be solved but as something to be accepted and shared rather than rejected or condemned.

The Fourth Industrial Revolution can develop properly only with the inclusion of Australian Aboriginal peoples, Pygmies, Taliban ... - not without them.

True soul consciousness is not exclusive but comprehensive; it sees everything as itself, as the divine consciousness; it sees all opposites as the wealth of the divine; it accepts absolutely everything as the will of the divine.

The more that awakened individuals exist who see the world this way - as a unity of all opposites and differences - the greater will be our collective awakening.

Without soul consciousness in people, there can only be collective madness.

DOES EVERYONE NEED TO WAKE UP

Not all human souls are meant to awaken. Each soul has a unique karmic program that determines the experiences they are meant to have in their physical body.

Many individuals are not interested in the idea of awakening, content with their current level of consciousness, which is predetermined by their karmic program. Attempting to awaken these individuals may result in resistance, as they are satisfied with their current state. They only want to get relief from hardships, not true awakening. The karmic program dictates the nature of the body and the conditions of life, which in turn influence the consciousness of the soul.

Each soul's self-awareness is unique, leading to diverse experiences. Karmic maturation occurs over several lifetimes, with the first phase being the collection of experiences and the second phase involving the soul's liberation from illusions and awakening. Souls with a stronger awareness of themselves and the divine belong to the second phase, as they are more mature and see the nature of things clearly. They function effectively and creatively, with the physical body having a weaker hold on them. In contrast, those with weaker self-awareness have a stronger attachment to the physical body and to the apparent physical world, requiring more experience and learning to find their way.

Karma means deed or work. As long as we have the illusion that we are doing something "with our body" in the world that is outside of us, and not that everything is done by the divine consciousness within itself and that we are that consciousness, we remain enslaved by karma and have karmic dramas, i.e. we are born into bodies and we go through our lives as if in a dream.

All these differences are actually part of the divine plan to manifest all that can be manifested, to be all that can be. The divine is all-that-is, it manifests itself as all-that-can-be. That is how the divine is actualized. It does this through human souls; they are the agents who carry out the actualization of all divine potentials on the finest plane through dramatic experiences of events and meaning. When the conscious subject, the human soul, connects the meaning of events and comes to understanding, then the divine consciousness actualizes itself. The deeper and more meaningful the understanding, the stronger the actualization of divine consciousness. It is most powerful when the soul realizes its true nature, the unity of the outer and inner world. This is then the complete actualization of divine consciousness or awakening.

That's all people do in this world. You are mistaken if you think they are doing something else.

This world is a theatre stage. As in any drama, those who play the main roles are few. There is a much larger number of those who have secondary roles, who are extras. However, their importance is equally important; the main character could not do anything without them. They are only ostensibly secondary, just as the main character is only ostensibly main. The whole performance is a unique whole with all the participants.

Only individuals wake up. Everyone else helps them with that.

There is no loss or injustice in recognizing that divine consciousness exists in all, regardless of their level of awakening. The awakened individual simply acknowledges this truth, while the unawakened may believe they are separate from the divine or lack its consciousness.

Divine consciousness is the creator, writer, and director of the theatrical production of life. Every being is inherently divine, merely playing a role with a persona or mask. The drama of life is timeless and has already occurred in the divine, with all potential events already existing. In physical reality, individuals manifest these potentials as they occur in the present moment. Despite the appearance of free will and linear time, everything is ultimately a part of the divine plan.

Even mistakes and those who make them are part of the creative expression of divine consciousness. The most unconscious and sinful individuals represent the greatest opposition to the divine, yet they are still a part of it. Recognizing the divine in all, even in the worst of situations, is the greatest temptation towards awakening. All individuals, saints and sinners alike, are played by the same divine consciousness. The difference lies in awakening, with the awakened being aware and the unawakened sleeping. This diversity and contrast within the divine is essential for its perfection and existence. As the universe is a hologram, the drama of life is reflected within each individual. The cycles of wakefulness and sleep remind us of the true nature of life's drama, with some individuals awake and others asleep, all part of the same whole.

This can be graphically understood if we imagine our life as a single line from point A, where our life begins, to point B, where it ends. The line itself is a series of points regularly arranged. Each point of that line represents one day and one night. By being born in the body, we reduce our consciousness so that we see only one point, the day we are currently in; we remember where we were and what we did, and we expect to see tomorrow.

When we awaken, we leave behind the illusion of linear time and the karmic drama. We see our entire life as one event, the manifestation of our divine consciousness. It happened as "our" life, but in reality, the whole already existed. We only dreamed it happened to one body, gradually, like something new, part by part, yesterday, today, and tomorrow, during the illusory time of our life. This is the view of the world and life from the perspective of soul consciousness.

As we mentioned before, the outside world is also our essence, our being, and we only dream that we are special individuals and that there is a world outside that is separate and alien to us. In reality, everything is one.

This means that the dream of the world only exists as long as the dreamer exists. All illusions about the world exist only as long as there is an illusion that there is one who has an illusion. Awakening is the disappearance of the dreamer, and this is how the reality of the world is revealed.

It also means that if we can be aware of both the outer and inner individual worlds, the appearance of their separateness, and the reality of their unity, then our essence, the essence of wakefulness, is beyond both. The essence of awakening is like a space that enables everything and is nothing of everything: both the world and individuals within the world, both reality and illusion, and the illusion of the one who is in the illusion and the one who is not. Such awakening is our essence.

When we say that our essence, awakening, or space is none of all that, it does not imply their separation from everything. Instead, the world and everything in it is precisely space itself, awakening itself. Space instantly turns into the world and all individuals, into all that is and into every subject that is aware of all that is. Therefore, when it is said that in wakefulness the world of objects and individual beings disappears, it does not mean that they really disappear, but only that they are recognized as what they have always been: infinite, unconditioned space itself, the divine absolute.

The true state of wakefulness dawns upon us when we apprehend that it has always constituted the sum total of existence itself.

The process of awakening is characterized by a cessation of the illusory perception of oneself as an entity distinct from this state of wakefulness.

The momentous event of awakening is precipitated by the termination of the dream-like state in which one perceives oneself as something other than what one truly is.

In essence, every account of awakening culminates in this epiphanic realization.

Epilogue

It is plausible that some readers of this literary work may harbor reservations about the plausibility of the experiences recounted herein. Perhaps the perspective on the world and the perception of human nature conveyed may seem too extraordinary, exclusive to the author. One may speculate that this is owing to my natal astrological chart, being born on December 22nd, with the Sun at zero degrees of Capricorn in the first house, in precise trine with Uranus at zero degrees of Virgo, and the Moon at the second degree of Cancer.

For those who hold this view of my worldview as fantastic, I would like to share an experience from my past that will elucidate what truly is fantastic. This incident convinced me long ago that the reality of human nature and the world is more extraordinary than the human mind can conceive.

In late 1981, on December 3, while I was in the realm of slumber, an incomprehensible force gripped me, abruptly halting my dream. Suddenly, a clear, mellifluous voice permeated every fiber of my being, resonating in the space around and within me. The voice called my name and reassured me that everything was in perfect harmony, and that I need not fret about my existence. It revealed that it had reached out to me to make known that it was within me, guiding me; that all that befalls me is in perfect sync with my evolution, and that I must accept it and become cognizant of it. "Do not seek outside yourself, everything resides within you," it implored. It also revealed that I carry the essence of all that exists within me, and that I will unveil it in accordance with my maturity, in harmony with time.

As my astral body was entirely paralyzed, I could only muster the question spontaneously in my mind: "Is this my higher consciousness? What does it resemble?" The voice replied that it was indeed my higher consciousness, and that it resembled me, like any other human being. At that juncture, I sensed that it was overseeing the karmic development of humanity.

During that time, about one minute, while this strange encounter was going on neither awake nor in sleep, I was completely paralyzed by a very powerful force.

Then I found myself in my room, in my physical body. When I got up to record the conversation, I felt someone's presence that radiated energy so strongly that my body froze from its influence. Although I did not see anyone, I knew exactly where he was from the strong energy presence, that some invisible or transparent person was within reach before me. From the intense bliss and awe that followed the whole event, I knew something good was happening to me.

One month later, as the memory of the extraordinary event began to dissipate and my mundane existence resumed its course, a wise elder materialized in my waking reverie, sporting a beatific, childlike grin in his eyes. During three encounters, he tutored me in the art of meditation, a practice that I later learned bears a striking resemblance to the *zazen* and *vipassana* approaches to self-realization. I committed to practicing this discipline daily. Several months later, I chanced upon a photograph of my guru from my dream and confirmed his earthly existence. Beneath the image was a name unfamiliar to my ears: Bhagavan Sri Ramana Maharshi.

After the incident I've recounted, my life transformed into a delightful game of uncovering the hidden within the obvious. Every incident brimmed with purpose and messages that awaited only my deciphering.

One day, the enchantments vanished, and time halted once more. Just like during that dream, the unseen figure who had aroused me in my sleep showed up in corporeal form. In reality, I perceived his countenance: my body, every gesture I made, the people surrounding me, their lives and musings, every aspect of nature, all sentient beings, and the entirety of space and everything within it – it was him. My awakening was no longer a singular state of mind, but the reality of all existence. I was everything that was, and I was it.

So are you.

Now awaken.

Upon awakening, you'll apprehend that actuality is infinitely more marvelous than any fiction, and the highest divine truth is present in every moment, and you are that truth, and every moment is flawless.

Thus, awakening can only occur in the present moment, never in the future.

The flaws that beset you are merely indicators that you slumber and abide in a hideous dream. As everything is impeccable, these very imperfections serve to awaken you.

If the current imperfections in your life and in the world you inhabit don't inspire you to awaken, then nothing will.

Printed in Great Britain
by Amazon